STRING ART

By RINI JOSE

TUTORIAL FOR MAKING OF STRING ART

610 X 610 mm

Contents

ACKNOWLEDGEMENT

There are a lot of people to Thank who helped me to make this happen. It was a very difficult task for a person like me to accomplish this task: Writing and publishing a book. Thanks to all who supported and encouraged me to achieve the same. Very much thanks to everyone for all the help and support.

INTRODUCTION

String art is one of the art which doesn't require any special skills. But it is an art which need patience. Most of the artist is making string art by using string and nails. String art is one of the most satisfying art in the world. The main attractiveness of this art is as I have already mentioned, you don't need any high level training or knowledge to start doing the same which makes it very easy. The result is very satisfying even if it is a simple task to complete a string art design. Anyone at any age (not for very young kids) can start doing string art.

String art designs can be geometric designs or patterns like: String Art Circle Pattern, String Art triangle pattern, String Art Rectangle Pattern, String Art Square Pattern, String Art Star Pattern, String Art Pentagon pattern, String Art Hexagon Pattern, String Art Octagon Pattern. String art designs can be letters like names or individual letter art. String art designs can be some objects like heart (love), star, anchor, etc.

I have created this book for beginners who like to create beautiful string art. This book has all the tips and tricks to start string art as a profession.

TOOLS AND MATERIALS

There are lot of tools which can be used to make string art. But I have mentioned the most basic tools and materials so that anyone can start their own string art without any delay. I will be explaining about the tools later in this book while explaining the step by step process.

1. Wooden board : 2 X 2 feet (24 X 24 inches)

2. Pencil, Ruler, Protractor

3. Design diagram

4. Tape

5. Scissors (small)

6. Nails (0.75 inch)

7. Hammer (small)

8. String 0.25 mm thickness (silk thread)

CREATE PLATFORM READY FOR STRING ART

Wooden Board

Dimensions:

Width X Length X Thickness: 24 X 24 X 1 inches

Wooden Board Color:

Wooden board can be any color but the color should be opposite of the color of string, if the string is light-color then the wooden board should be dark-color or vice versa. It may not be possible to see the string art if the background is as same as the string color. You can use paint to color the background or you can wrap the wooden board by using leather sheets, fabrics, color paper, etc.

Wooden Board Type:

Wooden board should be lightweight but it should not crack while hammering the nails. It also should be hard wood because the nails should not come out while tightening the string.

Design Diagram

Draw the design diagram in a paper:

Don't draw the diagram directly on the wooden board because it will be very hard to remove/ erase the design once the nails are placed. The paper size should be 2 X 2 feet (24 X 24 inches). It doesn't have to be one single paper, you can combine/ Tape four A4 papers to get the size.

Marking points:

Draw a square with length 54cm and width 54cm. Find the center point of each side and draw lines connecting the center points. Draw the diagonals as shown below. Mark points on the design diagram for placing the nails the distance between the points can be 5mm to 8mm.

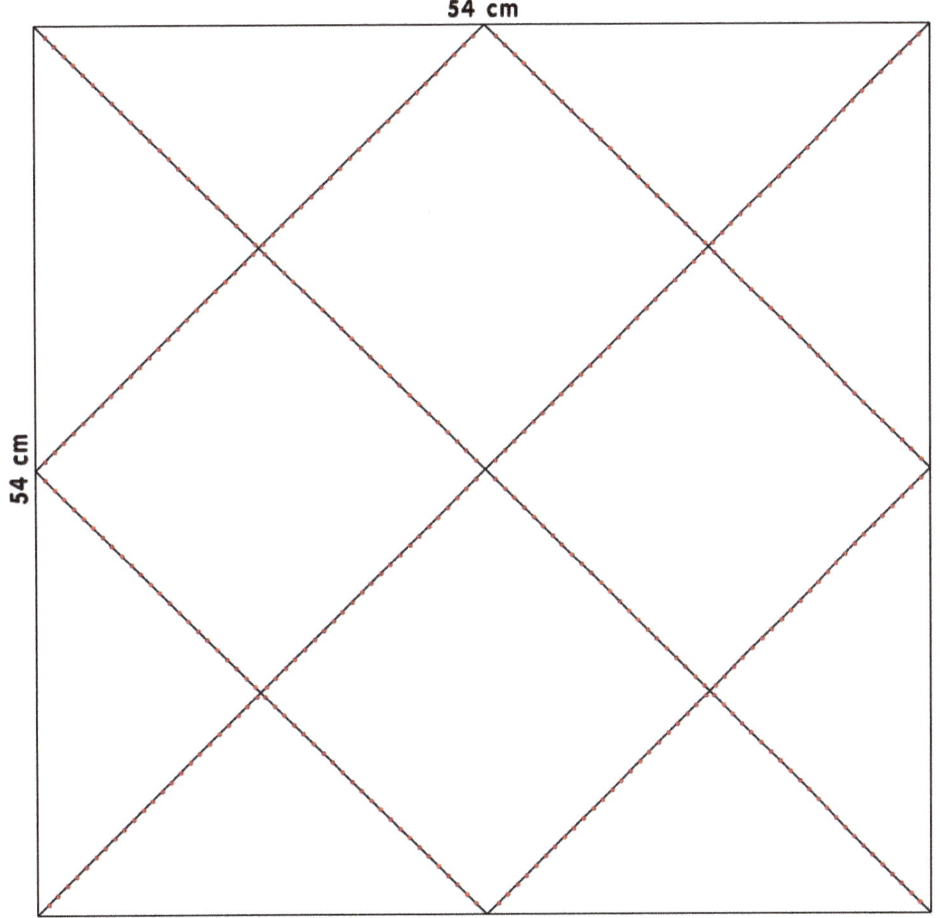

Tape the Design Diagram on the wooden board

Tape the design diagram on the wooden board so that it won't move while hammering the nails.

Hammer the nails

Hammer the nails into the marked points

Insert 30 to 40% of a nail into the wooden board otherwise it may come out while tightening the string.

Remove paper diagram

Remove the paper diagram from the wooden board once you have placed the nails. You will get a platform as shown below once you have completed all the mentioned steps.

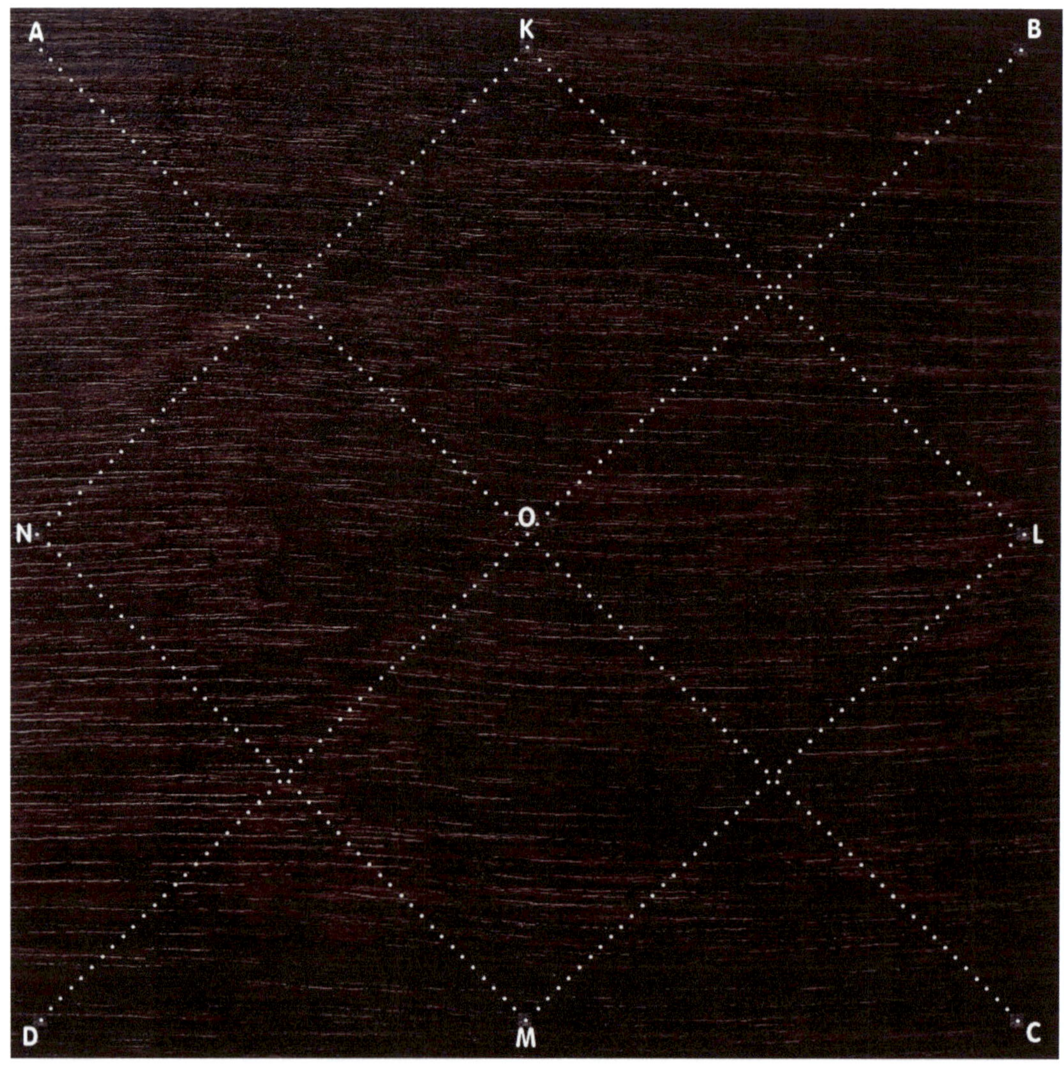

STEP BY STEP PROCESS TO MAKE STRING ART

You will get the final piece of art as shown below once you have completed the following steps.

Basic Steps

There are mainly 3 layers to complete this string art design.

String Art Layer: 1

String Art Layer: 2

String Art Layer: 3

String Art Layer-1: Step by step instructions

This layer has 5 parts. For the first part, start from Point-A. Find 19th nail (marked as A19) from Point-A. Tie the string onto that nail. Then, Find 4th nail (marked as N4) from Point-N. Connect the string from A19 to N4 as shown below:

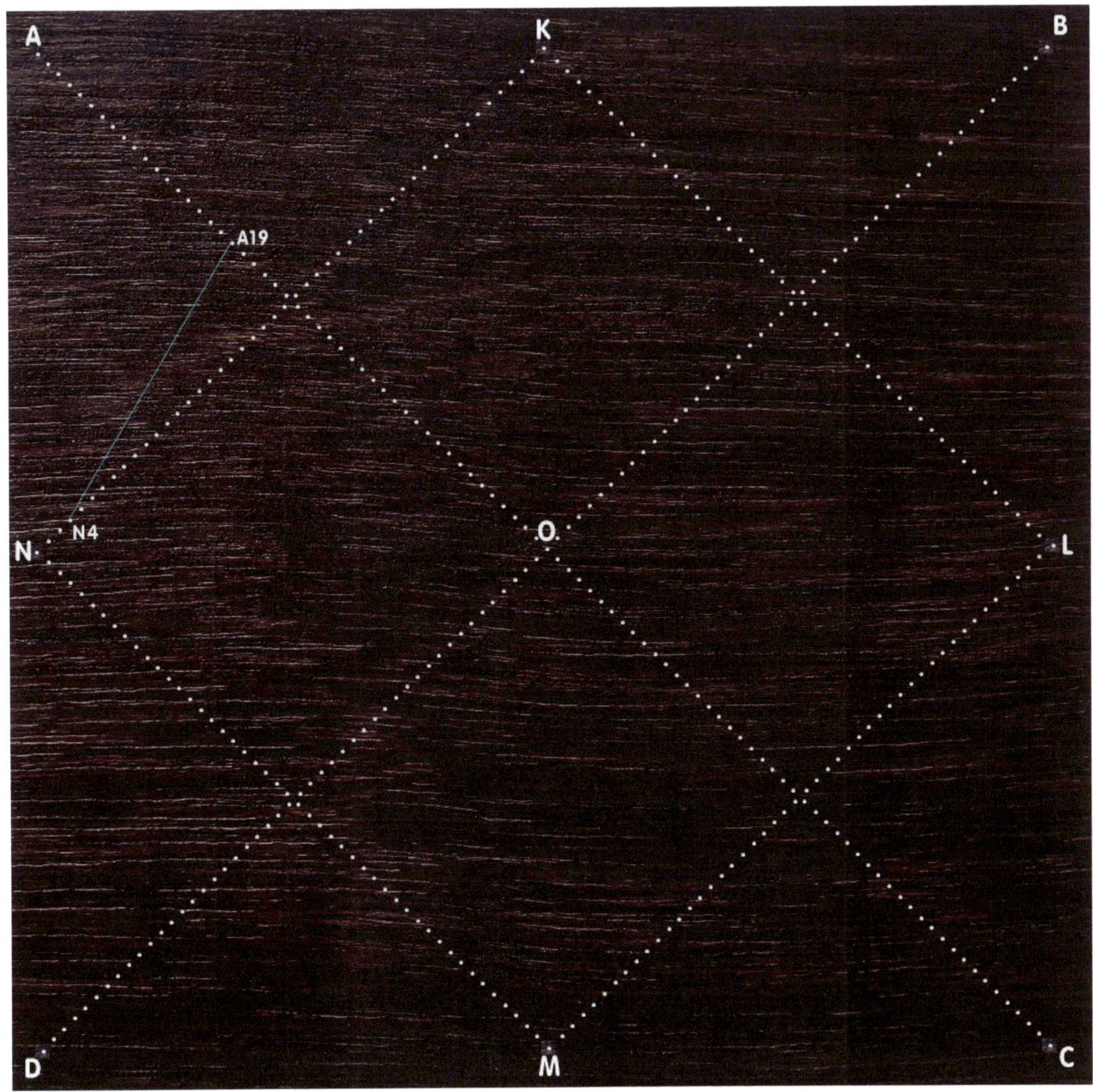

Wrap the string onto the nail point N4 and connect back to the nail point A18 as shown below:

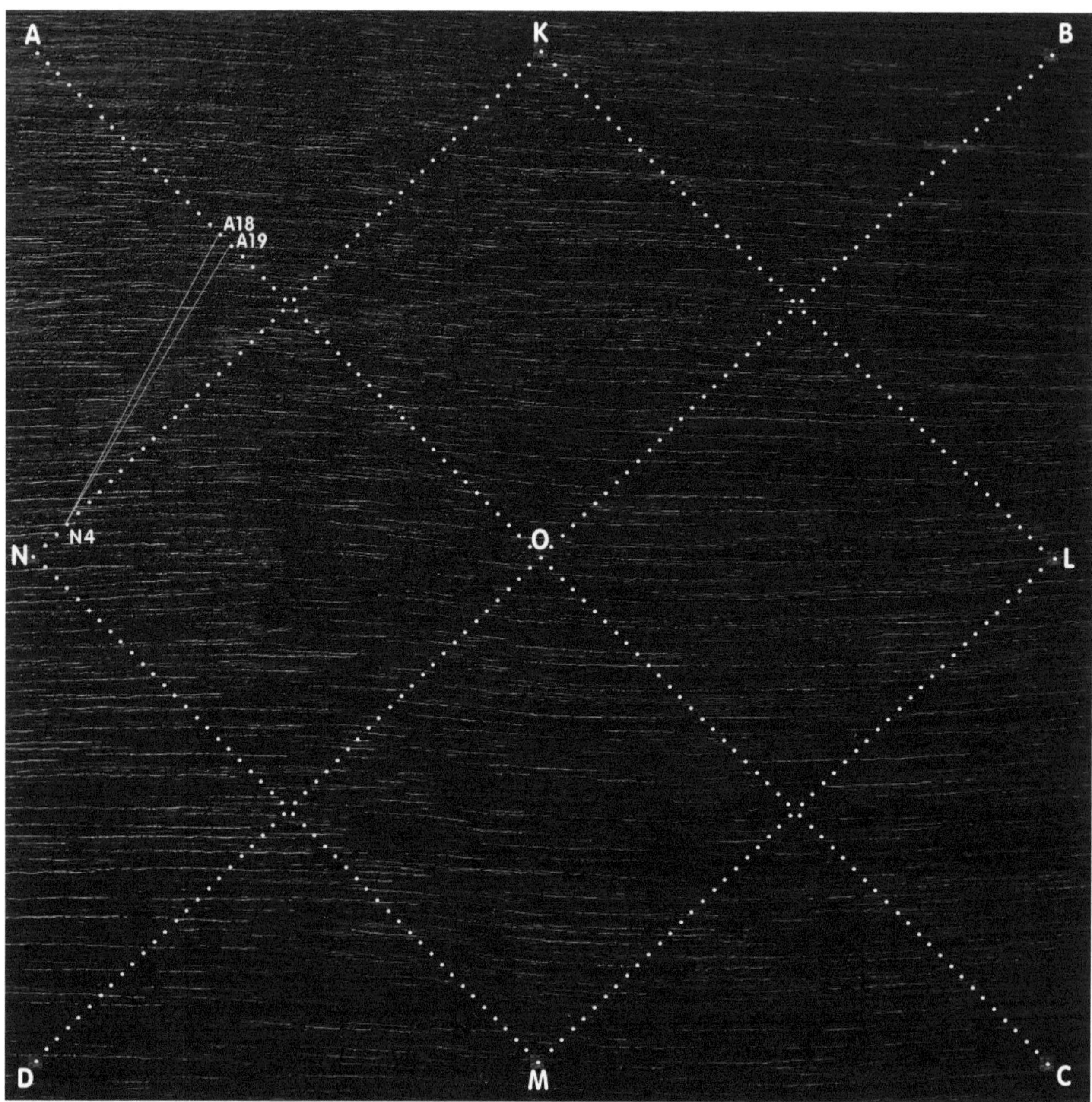

Wrap the string onto the nail A18 and then connect to the nail point N5 as shown in the picture below:

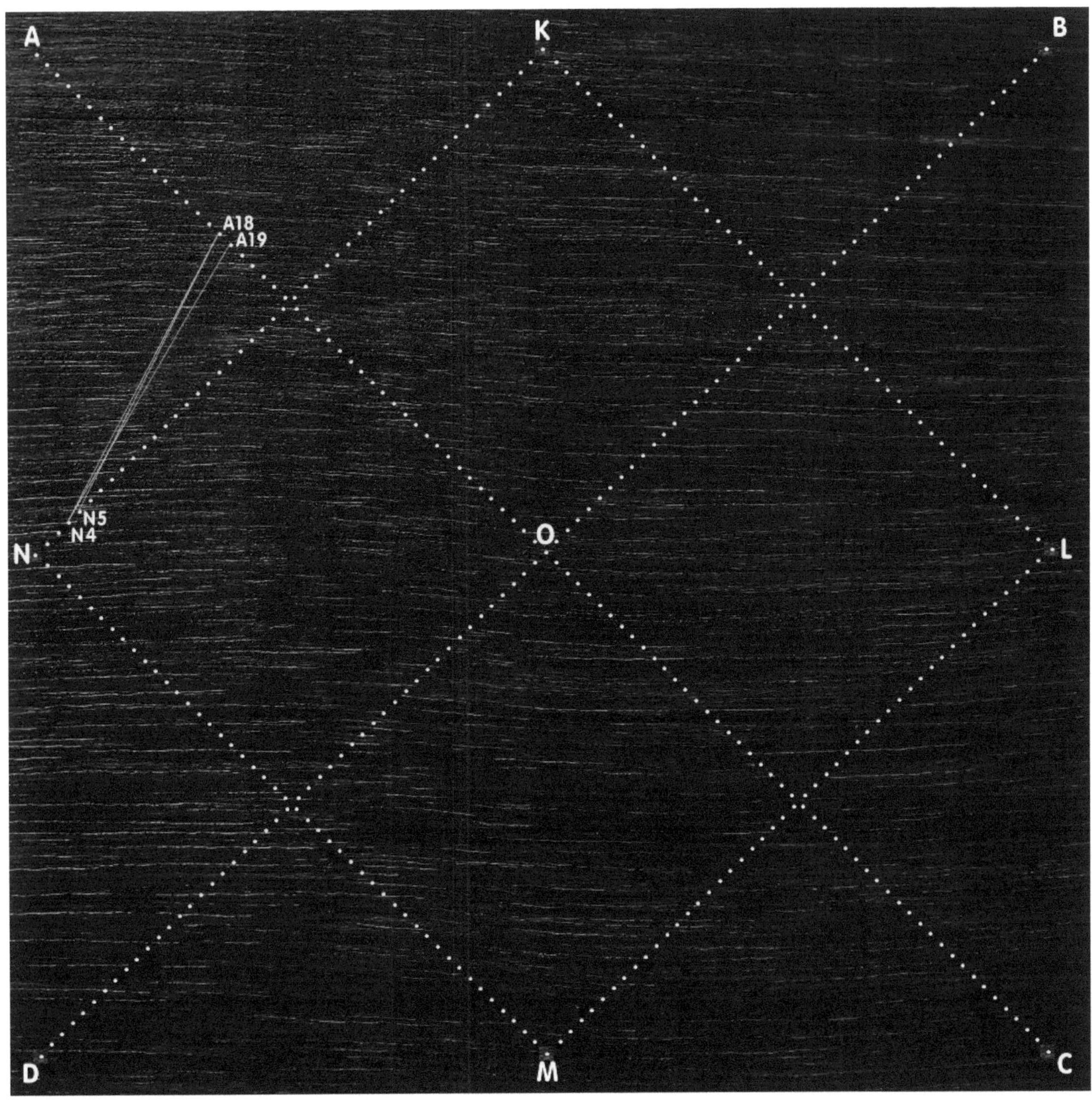

Wrap the string onto the nail point N5 and connect back to the nail point A17 as shown below:

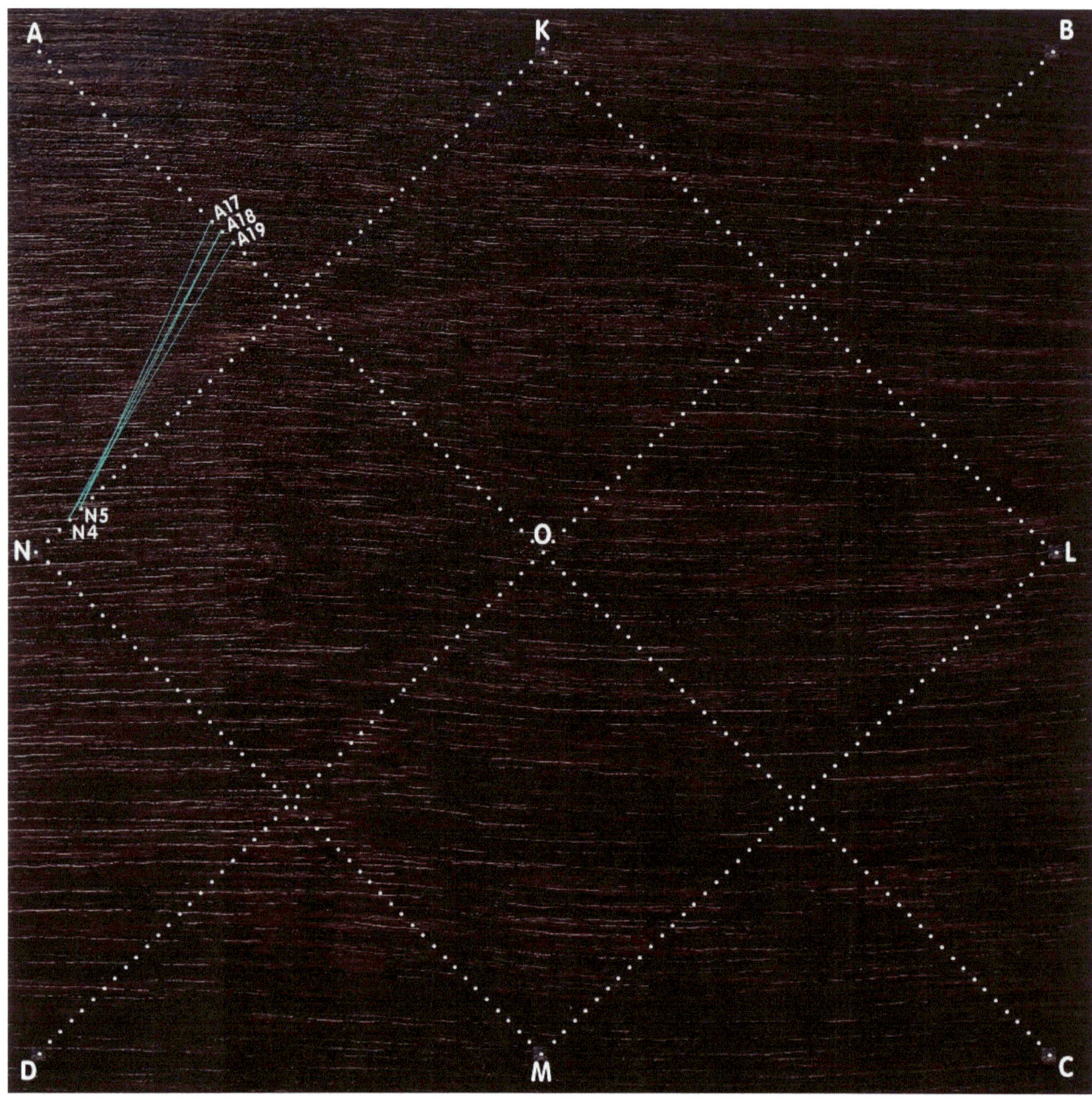

Wrap the string onto the nail A17 and then connect to the nail point N6 as shown in the picture below:

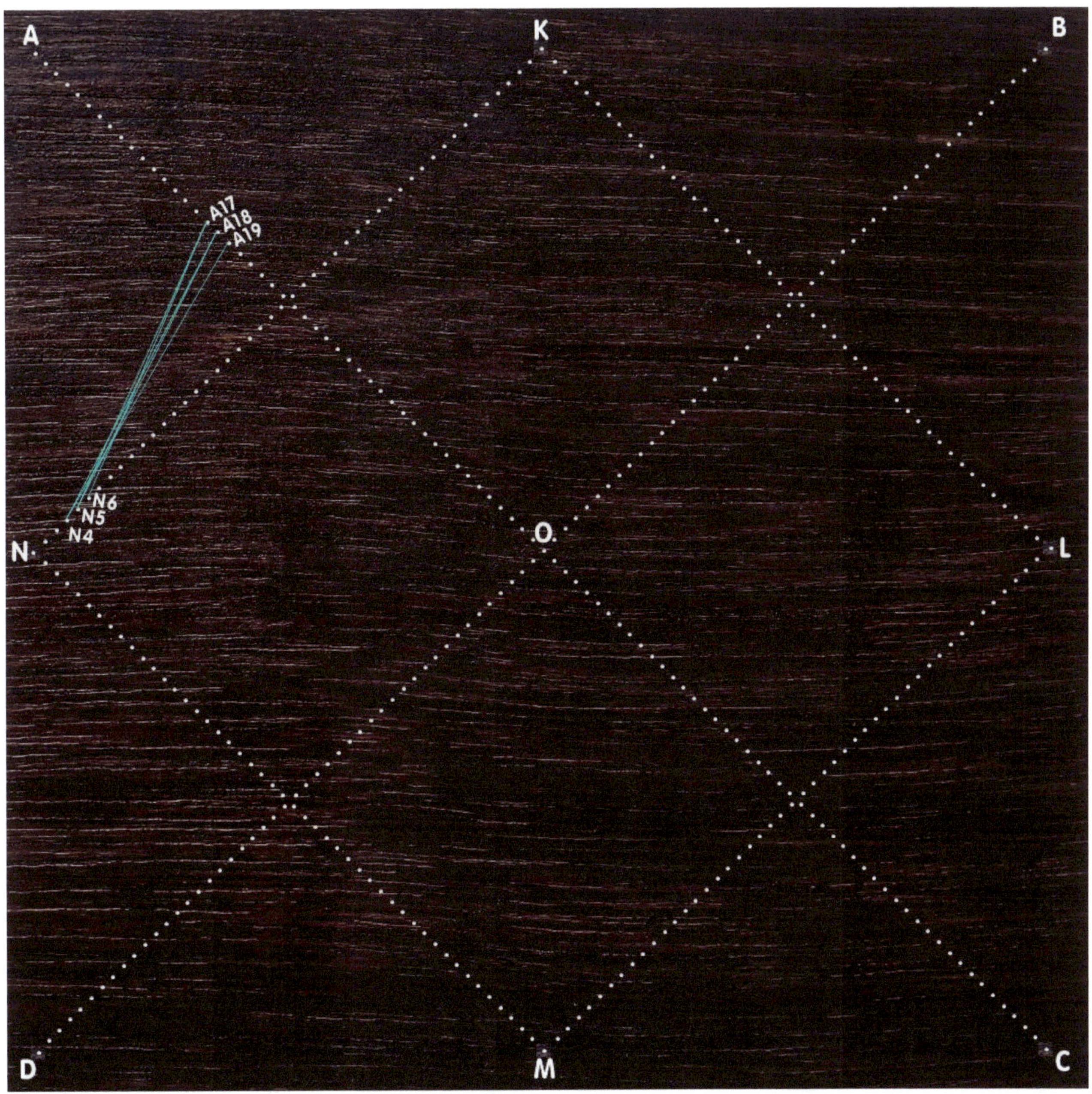

Continue this step until you reach the nail-point A4 from point-A and the nail-point N19 from Point-N. Tie the string onto that nail and you will get the result as shown below:

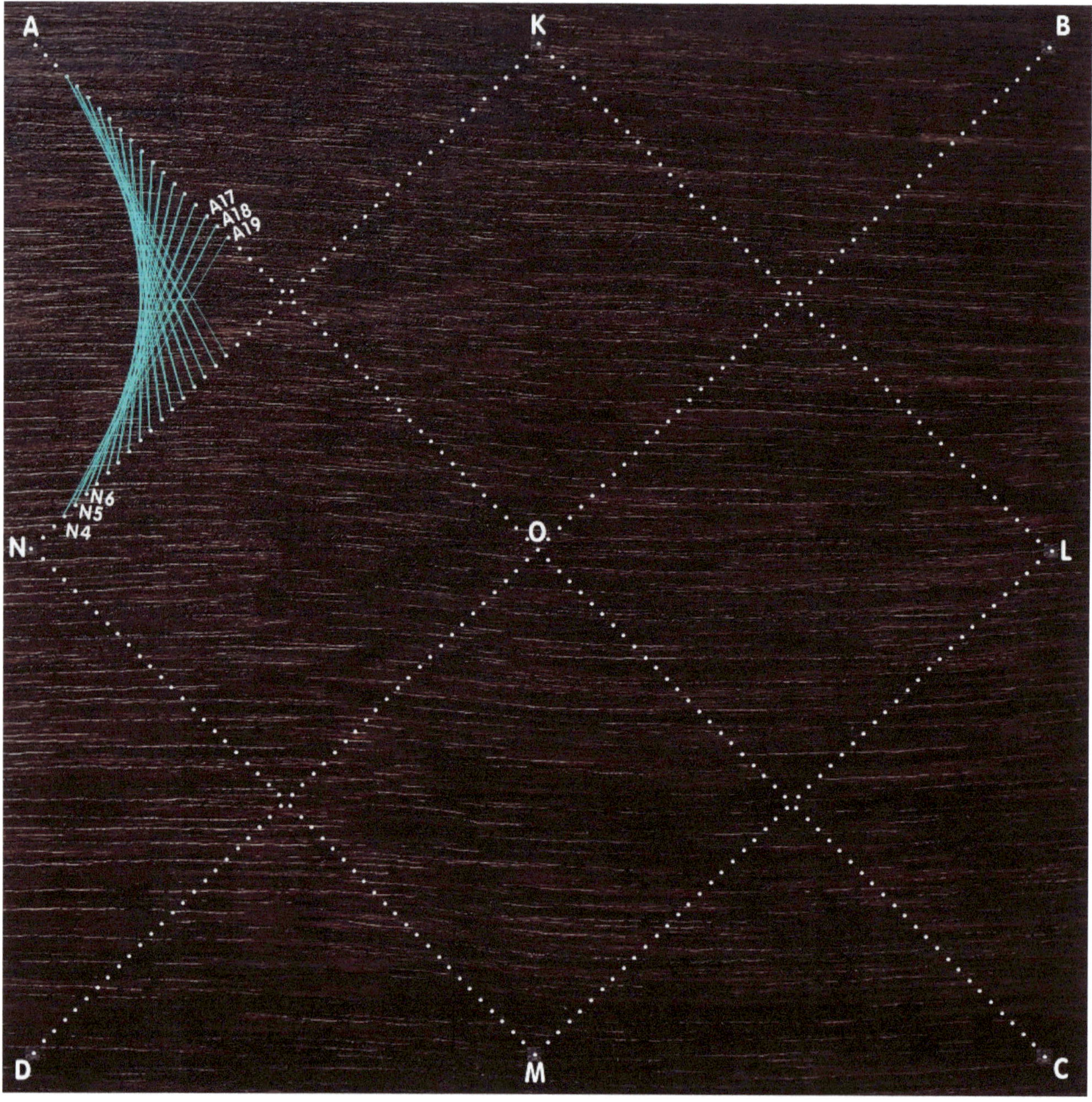

Repeat the same process in other sides of the square shape and you will get the result as shown below:

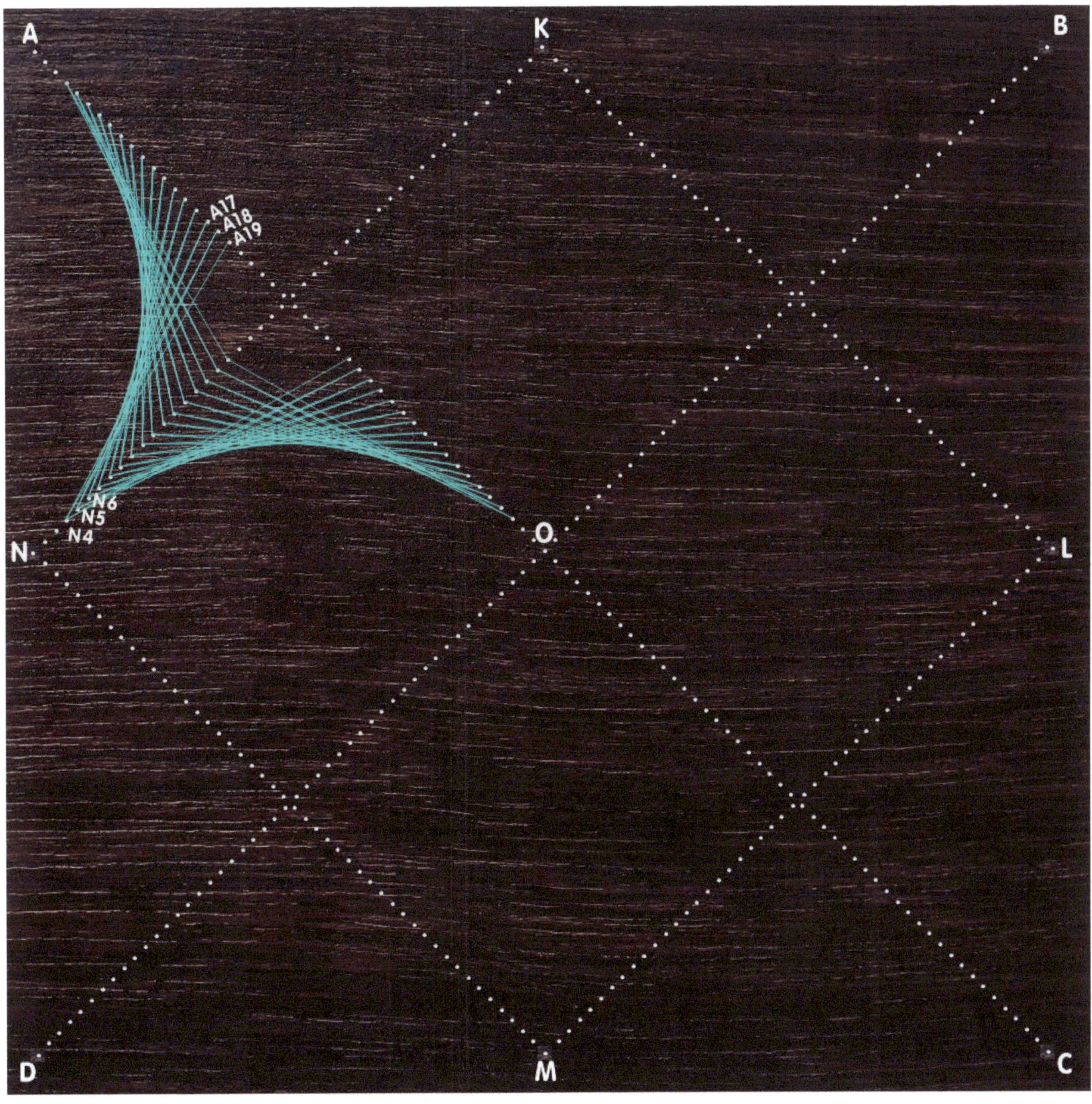

Repeat the same process in every sides of the square shape and you will get the result as shown below:

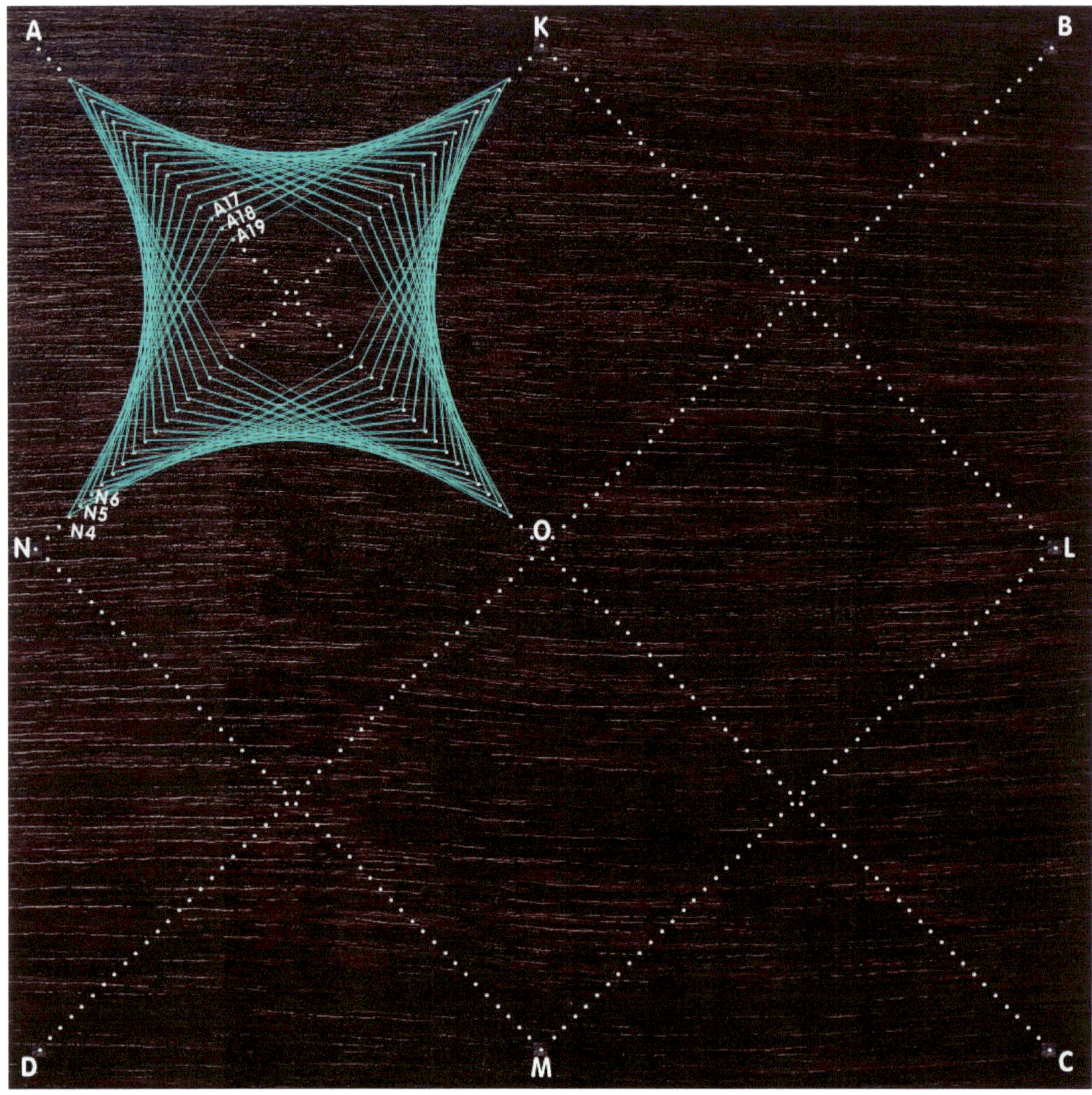

Repeat the same process in every square shapes in the design and you will get the result as shown below:

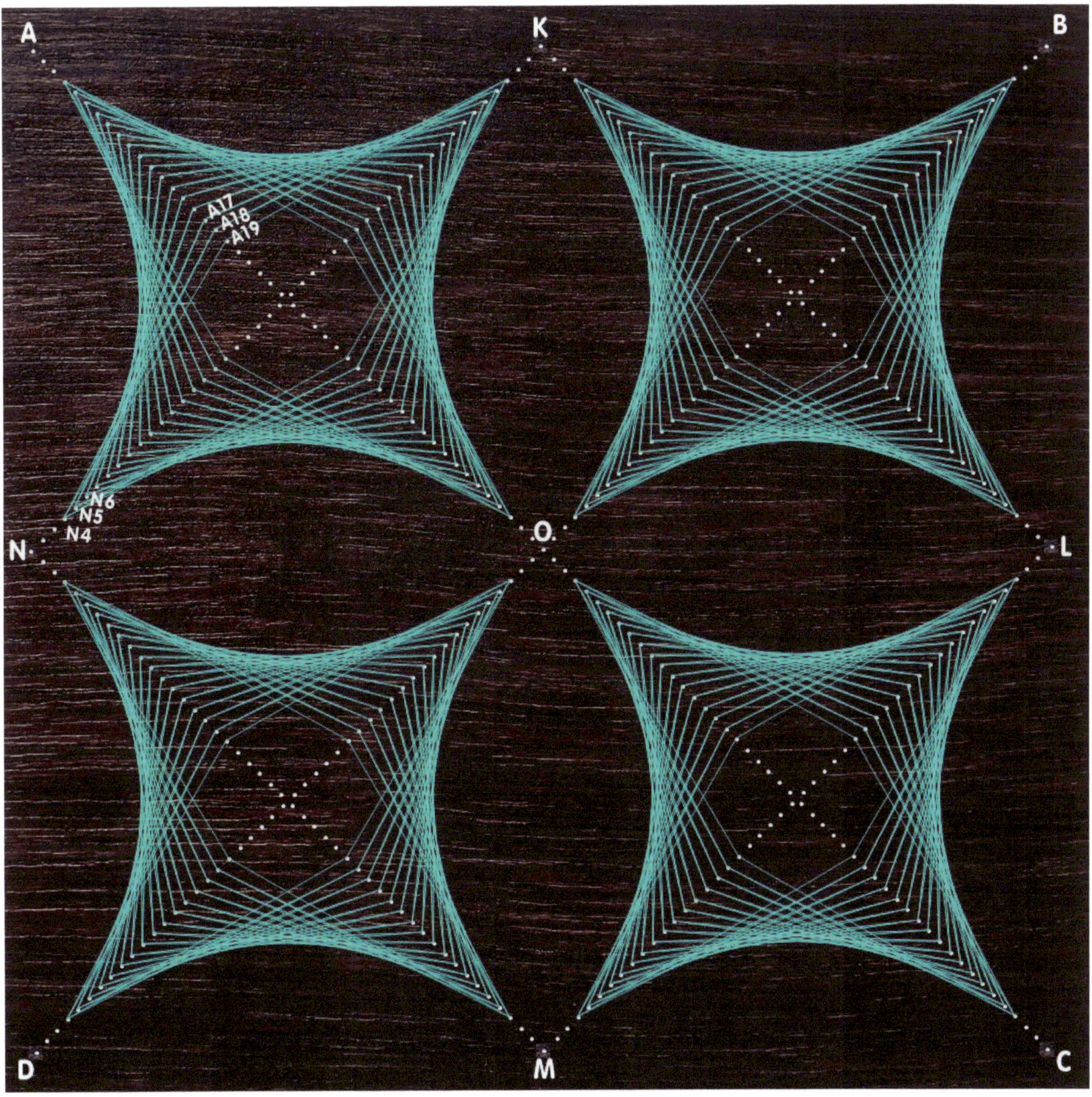

Also repeat the same process in the center and you will get the final result as shown below. This is the final result for Layer-1 in this design:

String Art Layer-2: Step by step instructions

This layer has 4 parts. For the first part, start from Point-O. Find 4th nail (marked as O4) from Point-O. Tie the string onto that nail. Then, Find 4th nail (marked as B4) from Point-B. Connect the string from O4 to B4 as shown below:

Wrap the string onto the nail point B4 and connect back to the nail point O5 as shown below:

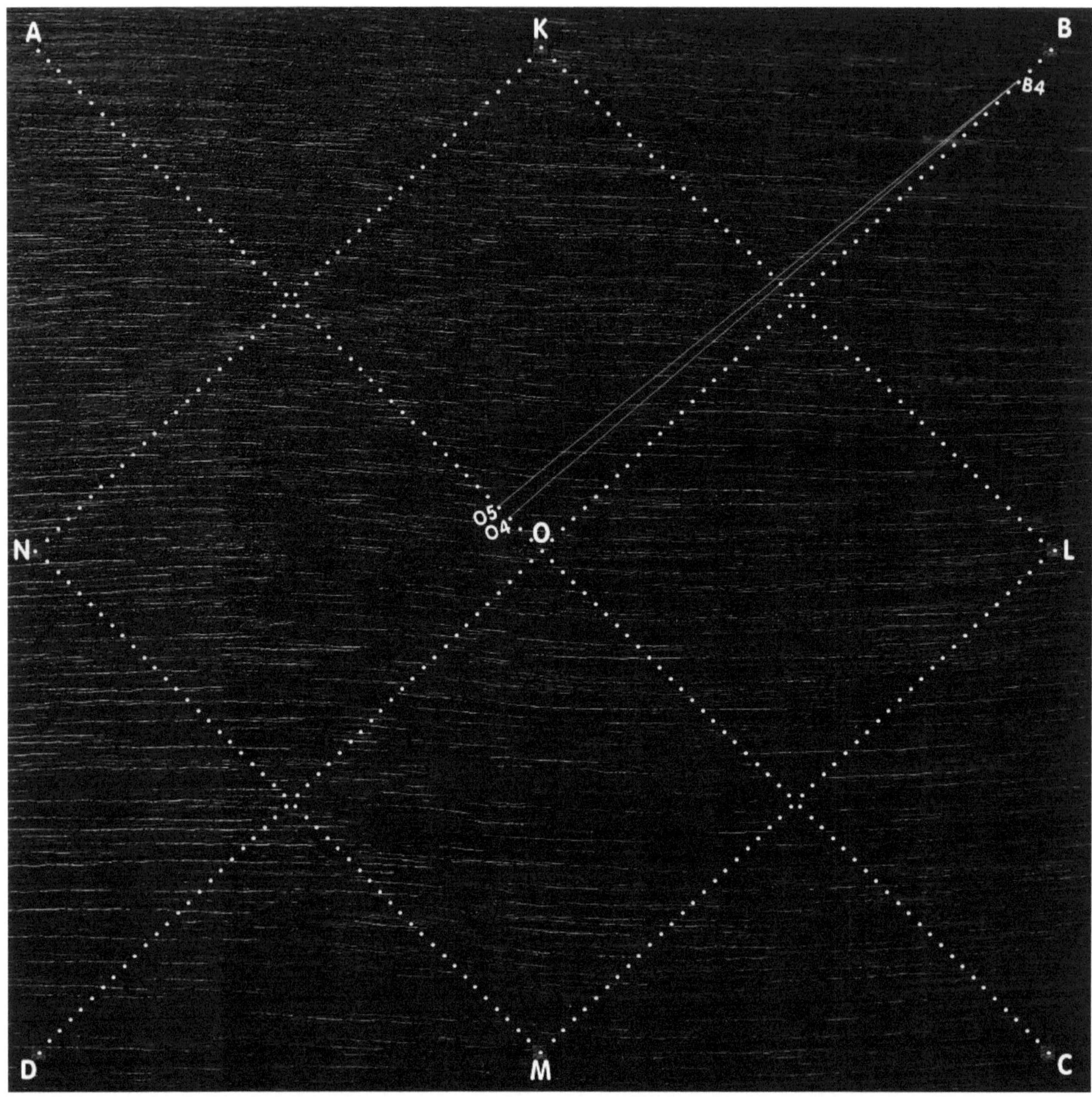

Wrap the string onto the nail O5 and then connect to the nail point B5 as shown in the picture below:

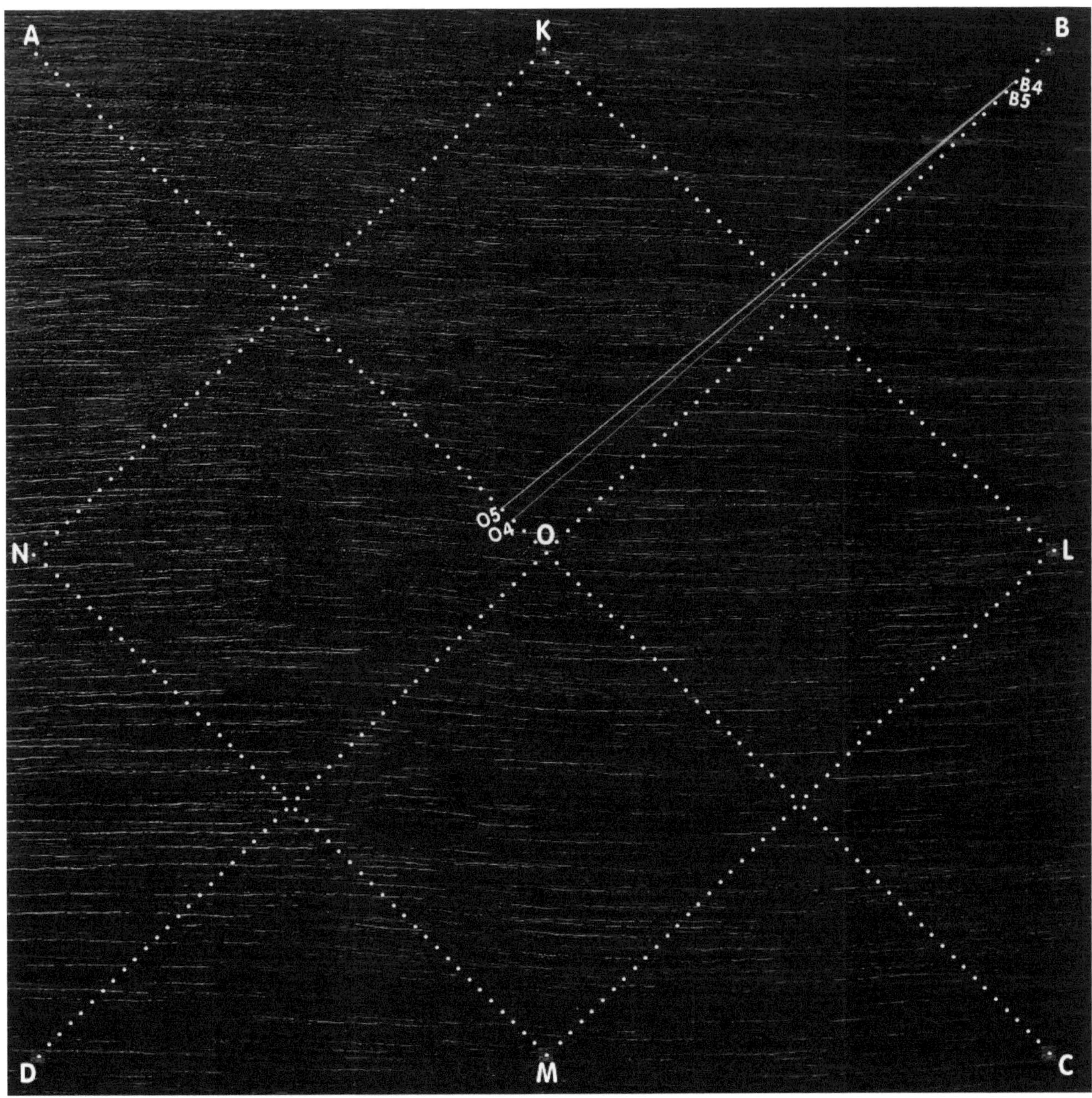

Wrap the string onto the nail point B5 and connect back to the nail point O6 as shown below:

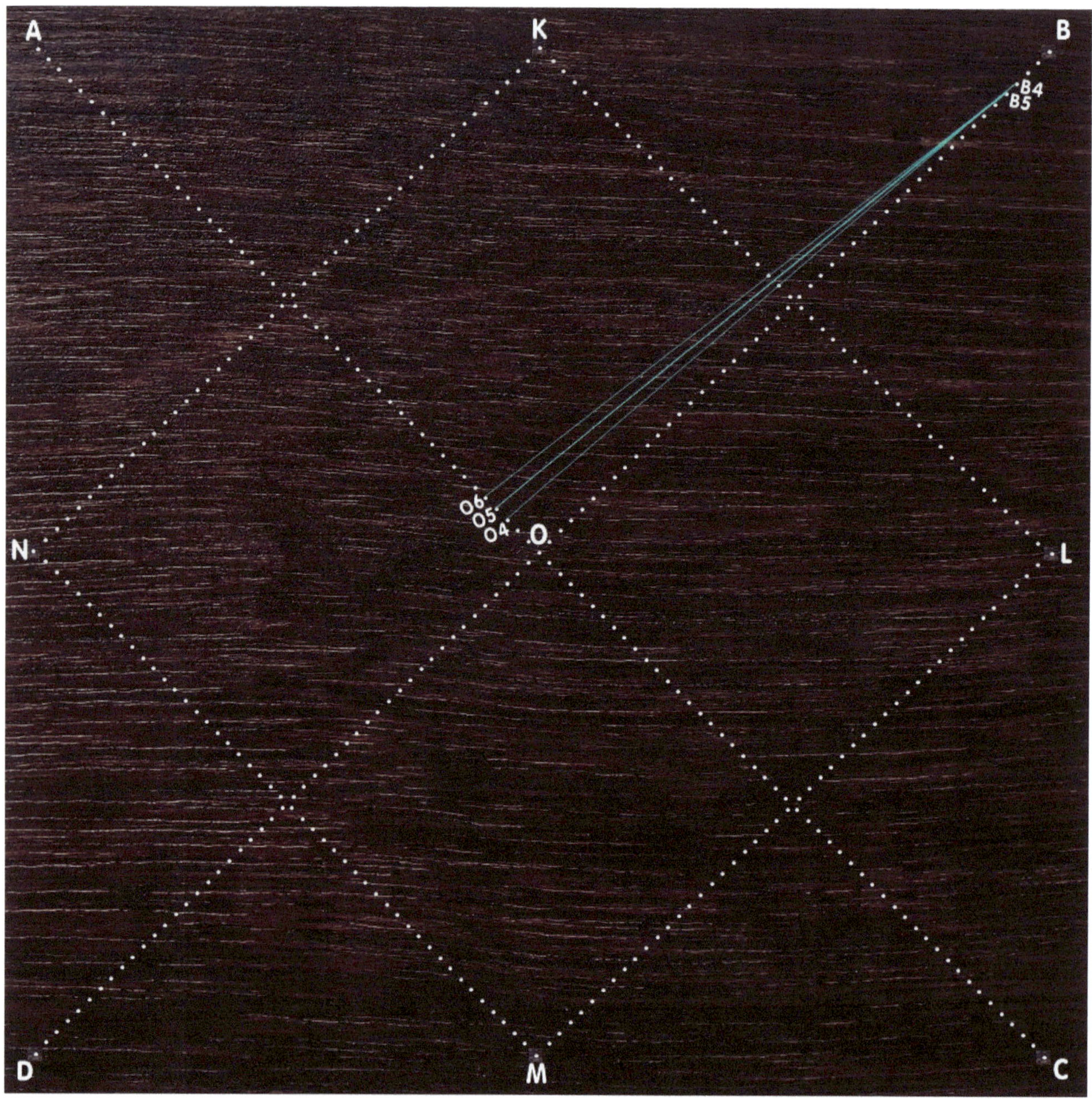

Wrap the string onto the nail O6 and then connect to the nail point B6 as shown in the picture below:

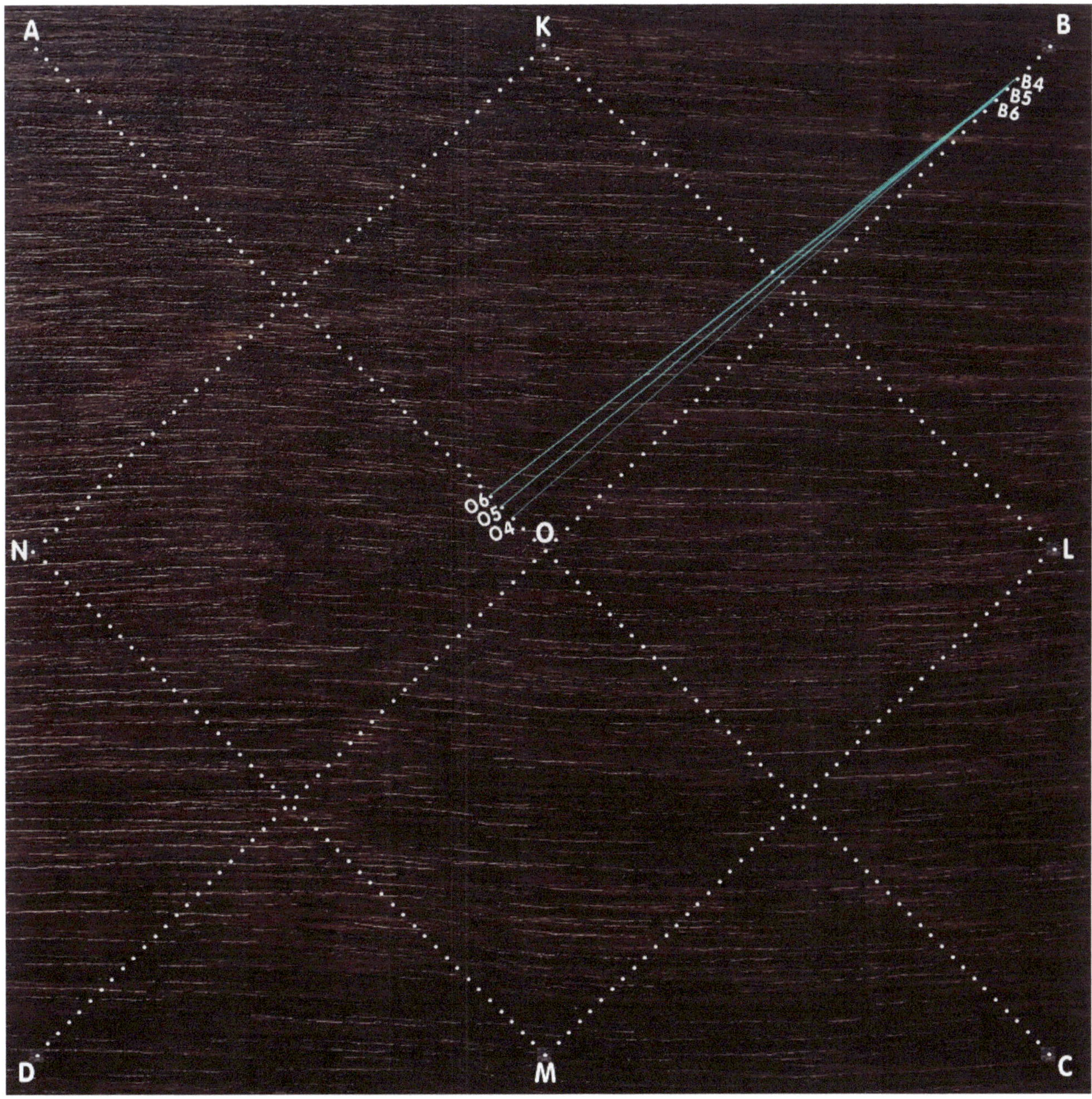

Wrap the string onto the nail B6 and then connect to the nail point O7 as shown in the picture below:

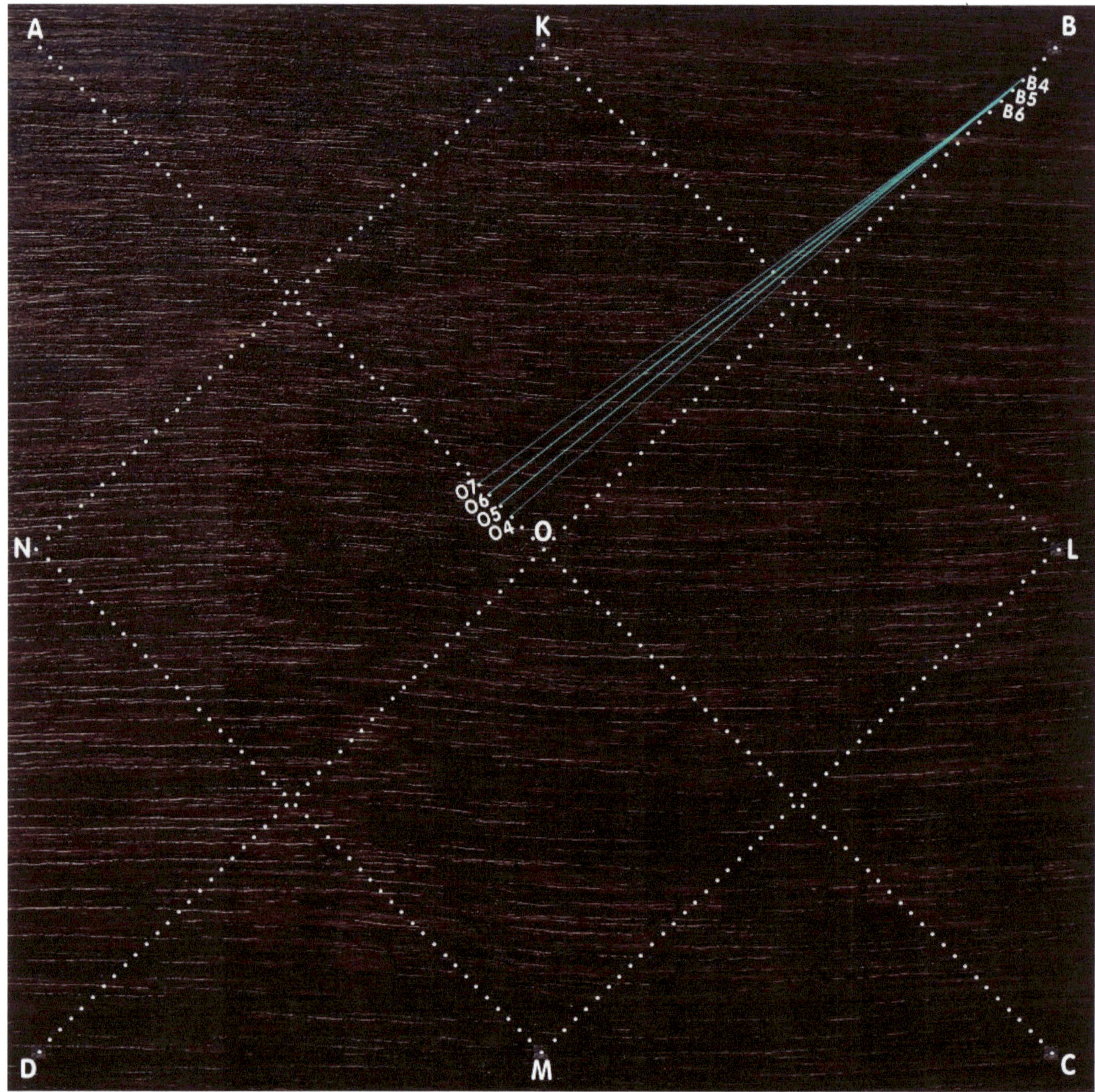

Continue this step until you reach the nail-point O19 from point-O and the nail-point B19 from Point-B. Tie the string onto that nail and you will get the result as shown below:

Repeat the same process in other side of the design and you will get the result as shown below:

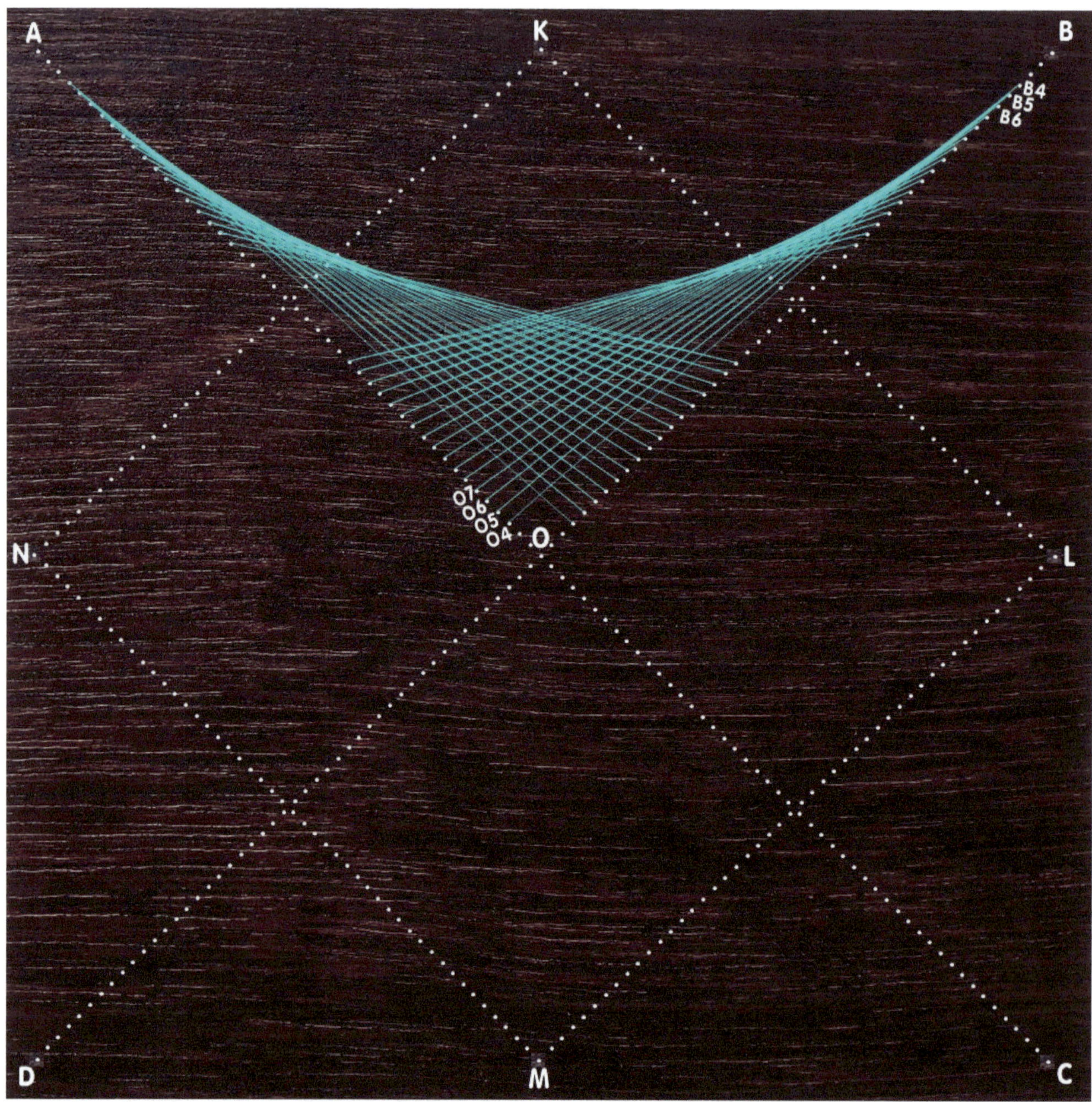

Repeat the same process in the right side (bottom) of the design and you will get the result as shown below:

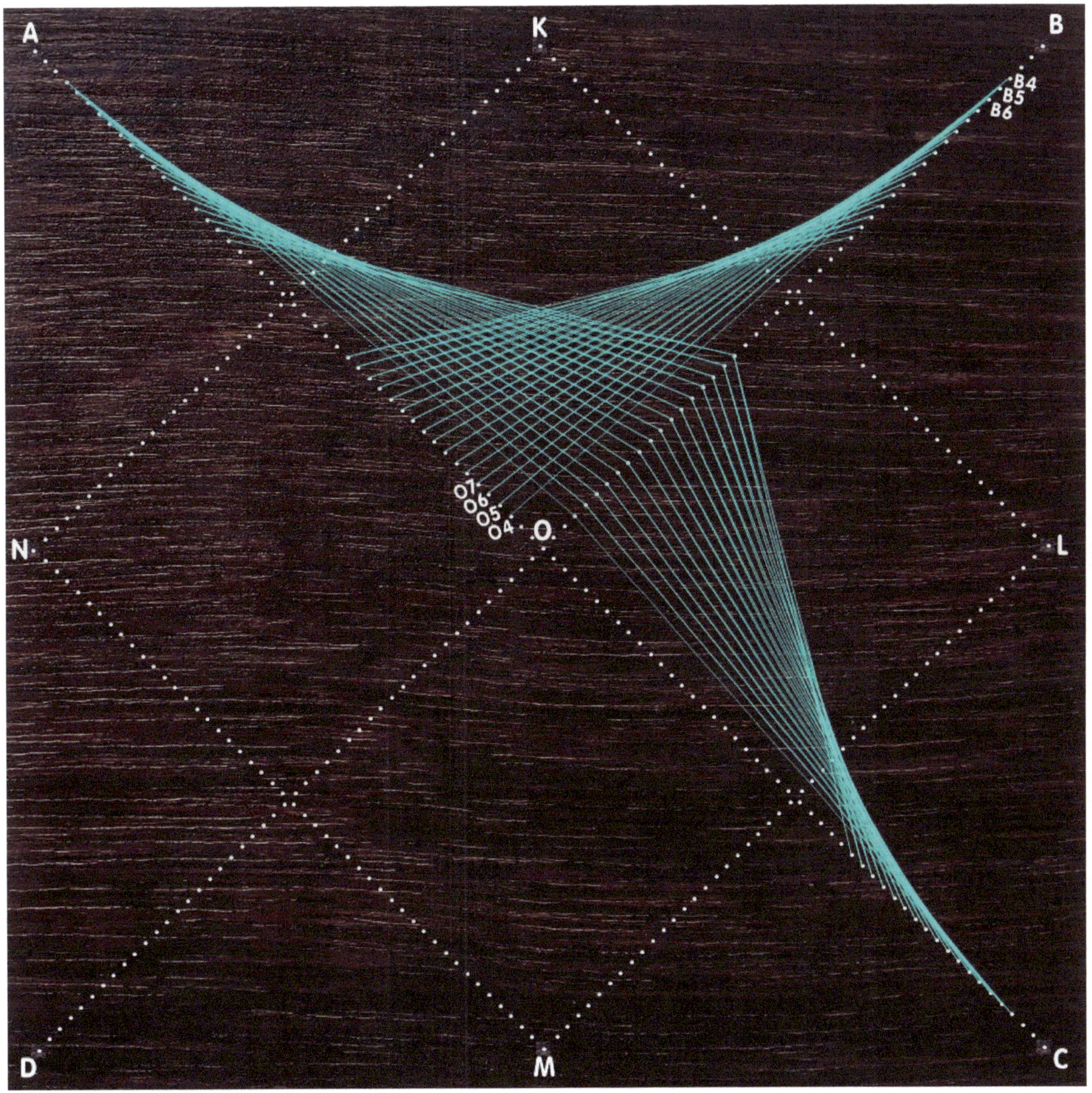

Also repeat the same process in the right side (top) of the design and you will get the result as shown below:

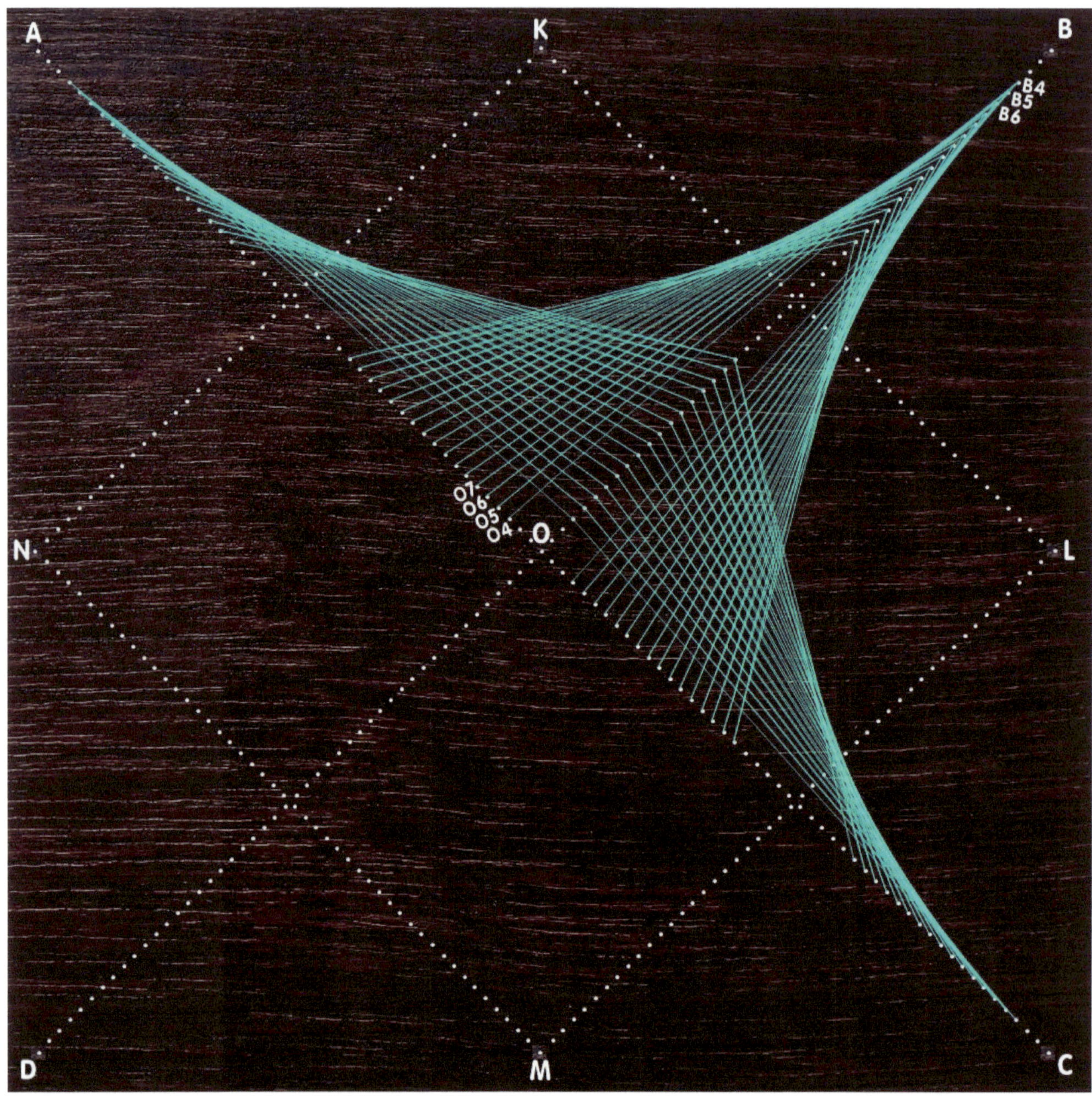

Also repeat the same process in all the sides and you will get the final result as shown below. This is the final result for Layer-2 in this design:

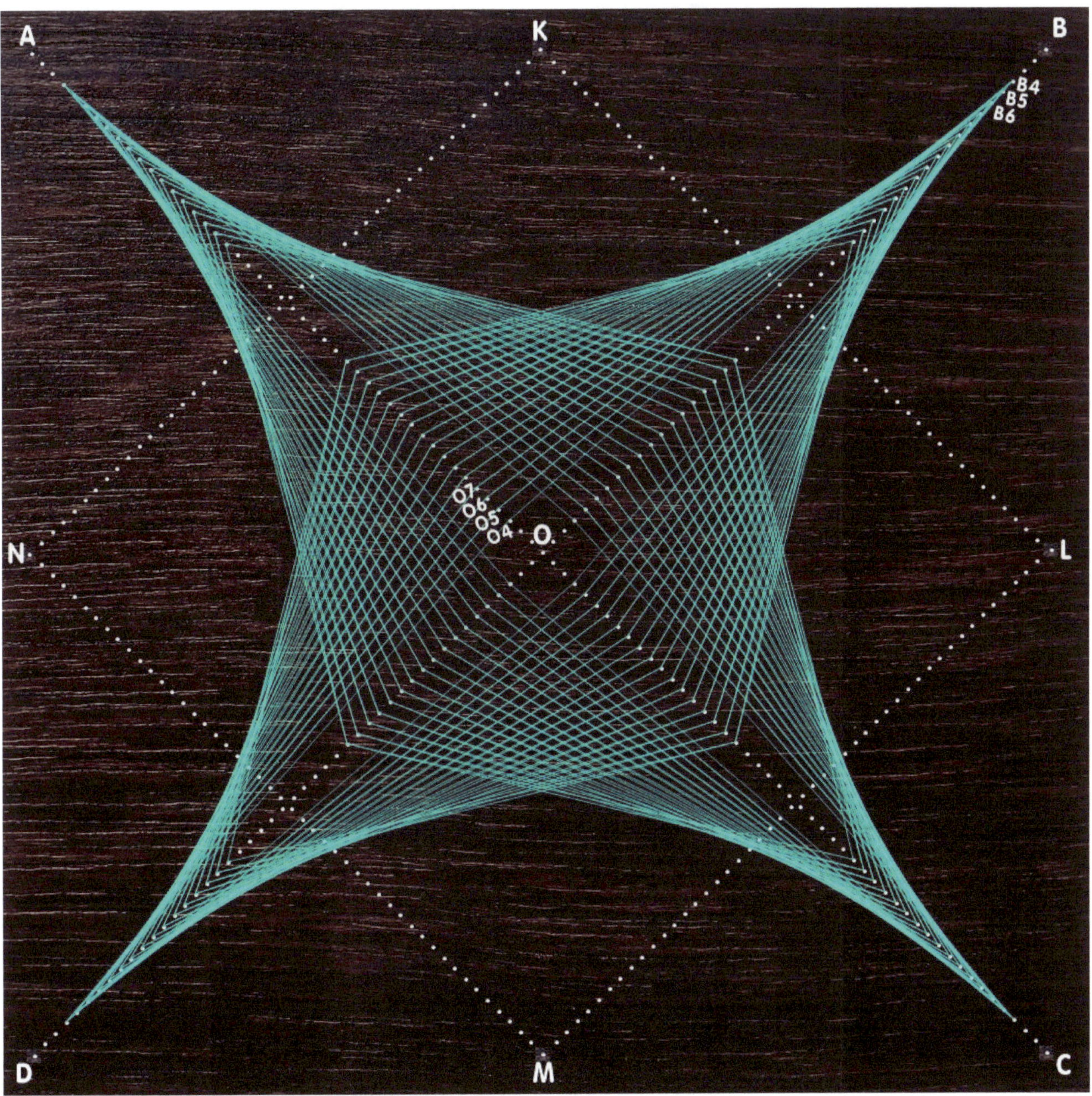

You will get the result as shown below once you have completed Layer-1 and Layer-2:

String Art Layer-3: Step by step instructions

This layer has 4 parts. For the first part, start from Point-O. Find 4th nail (marked as O4) from Point-O. Tie the string onto that nail. Then, Find 4th nail (marked as M4) from Point-M. Connect the string from O4 to M4 as shown below:

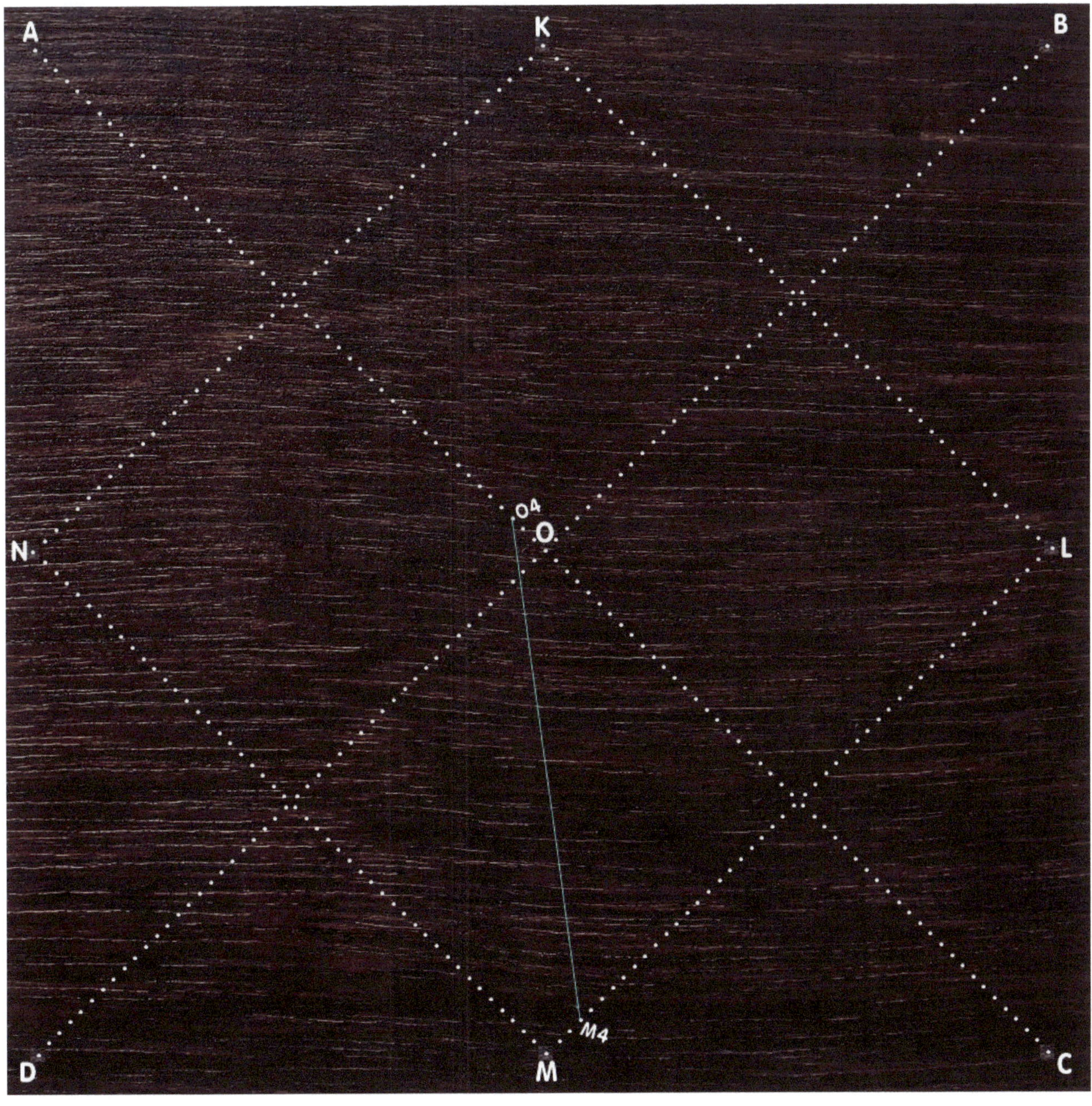

Wrap the string onto the nail point M4 and connect back to the nail point O5 as shown below:

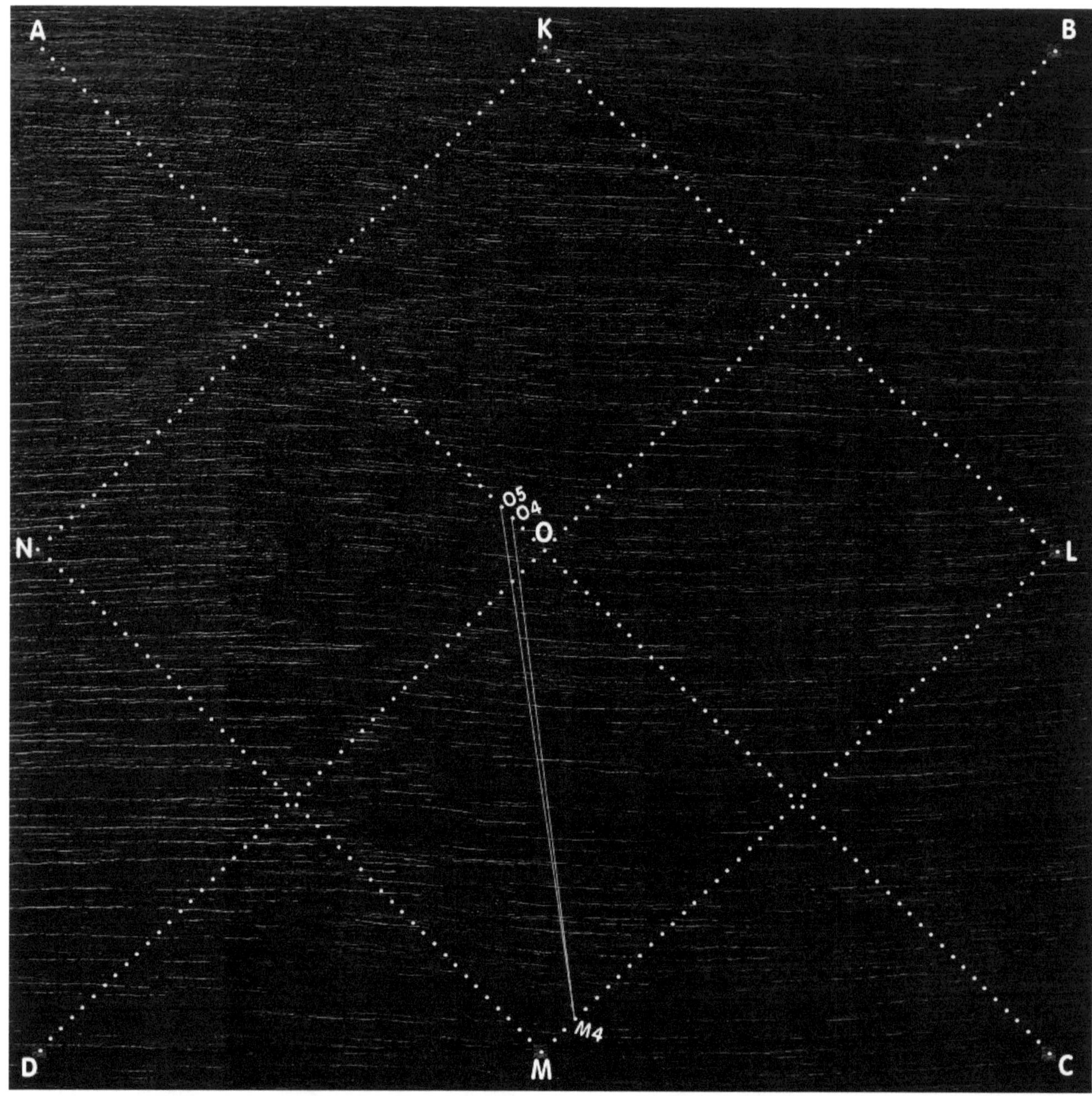

Wrap the string onto the nail O5 and then connect to the nail point M5 as shown in the picture below:

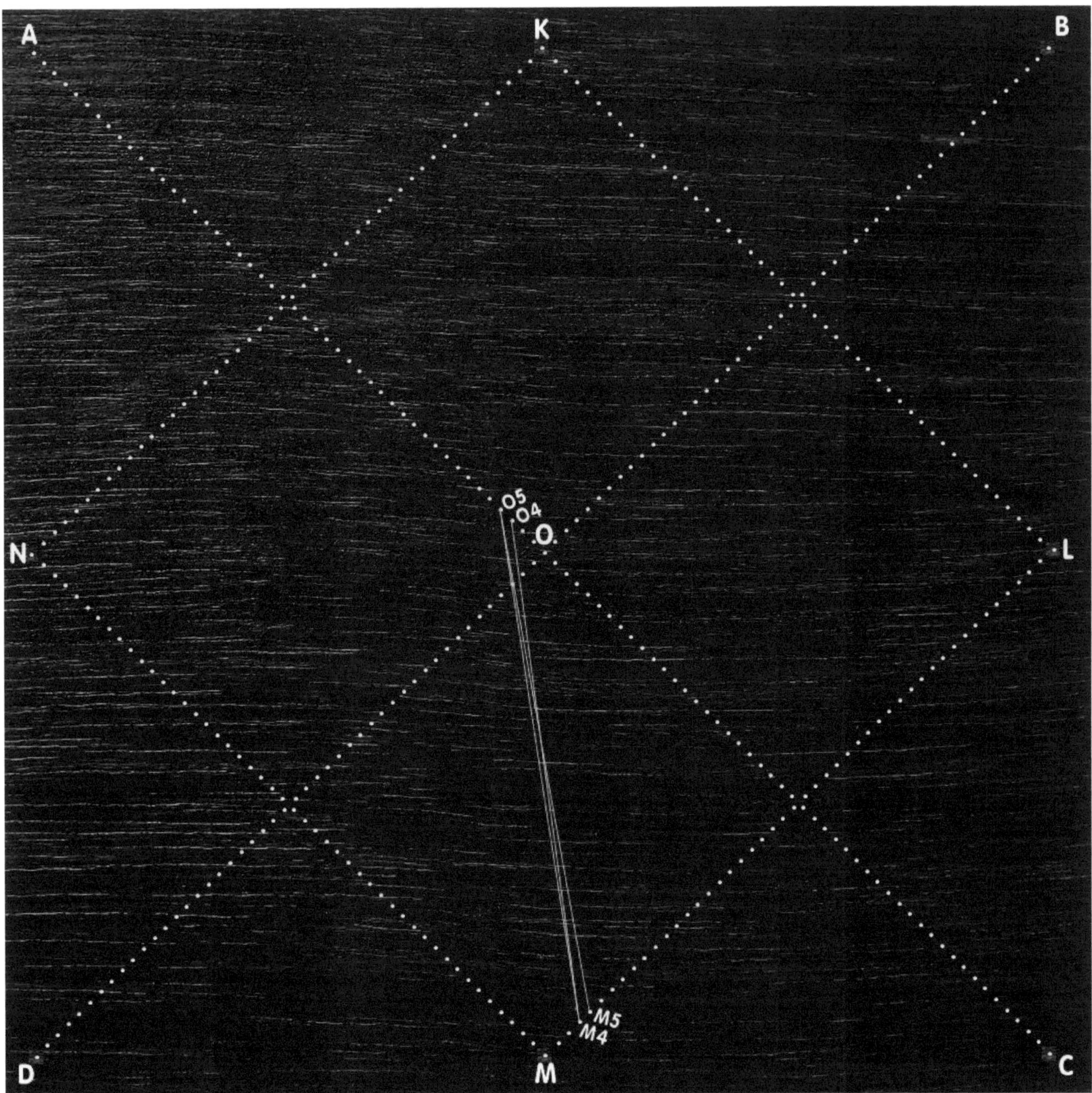

Wrap the string onto the nail point M5 and connect back to the nail point O6 as shown below:

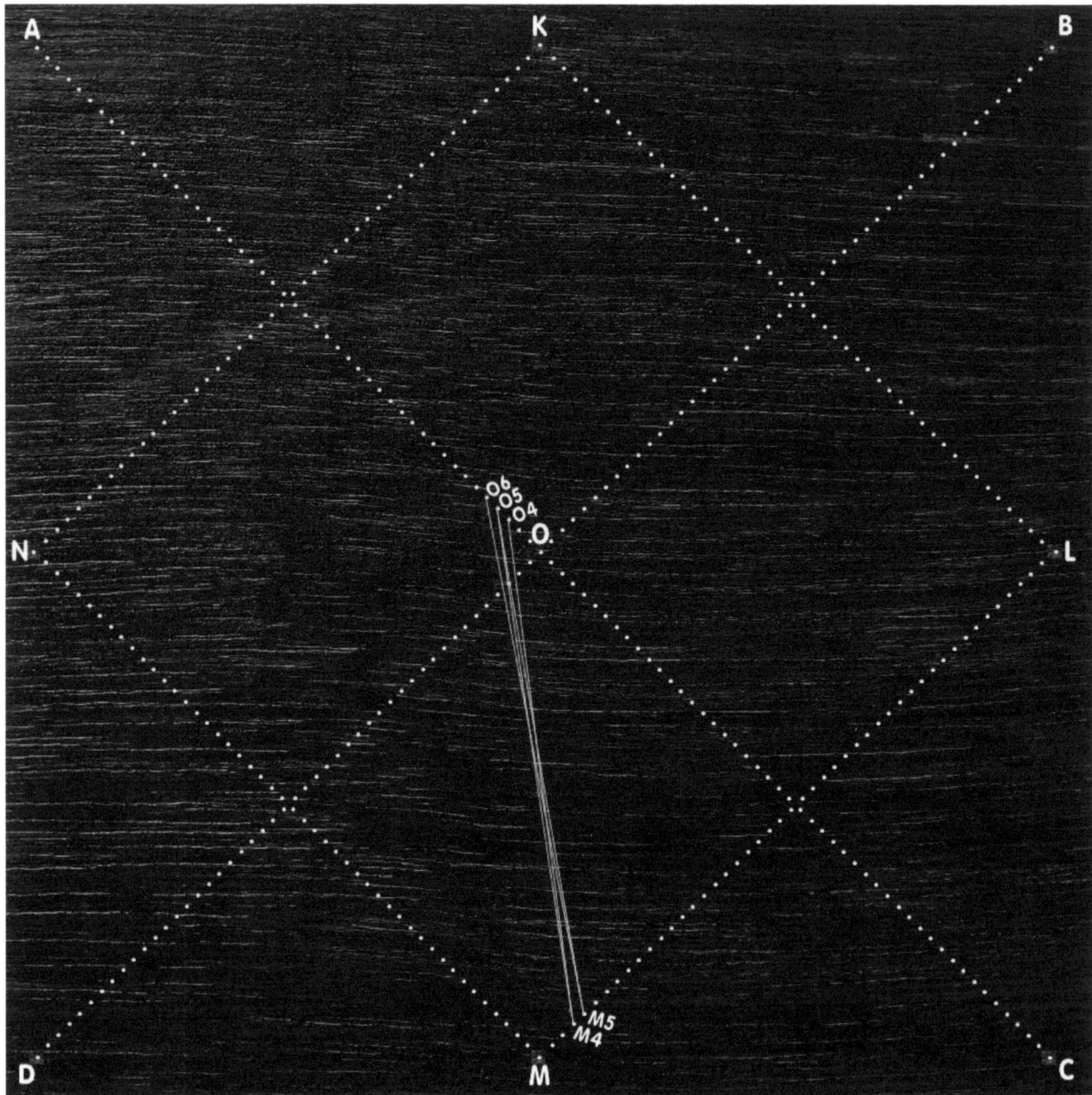

Wrap the string onto the nail O6 and then connect to the nail point M6 as shown in the picture below:

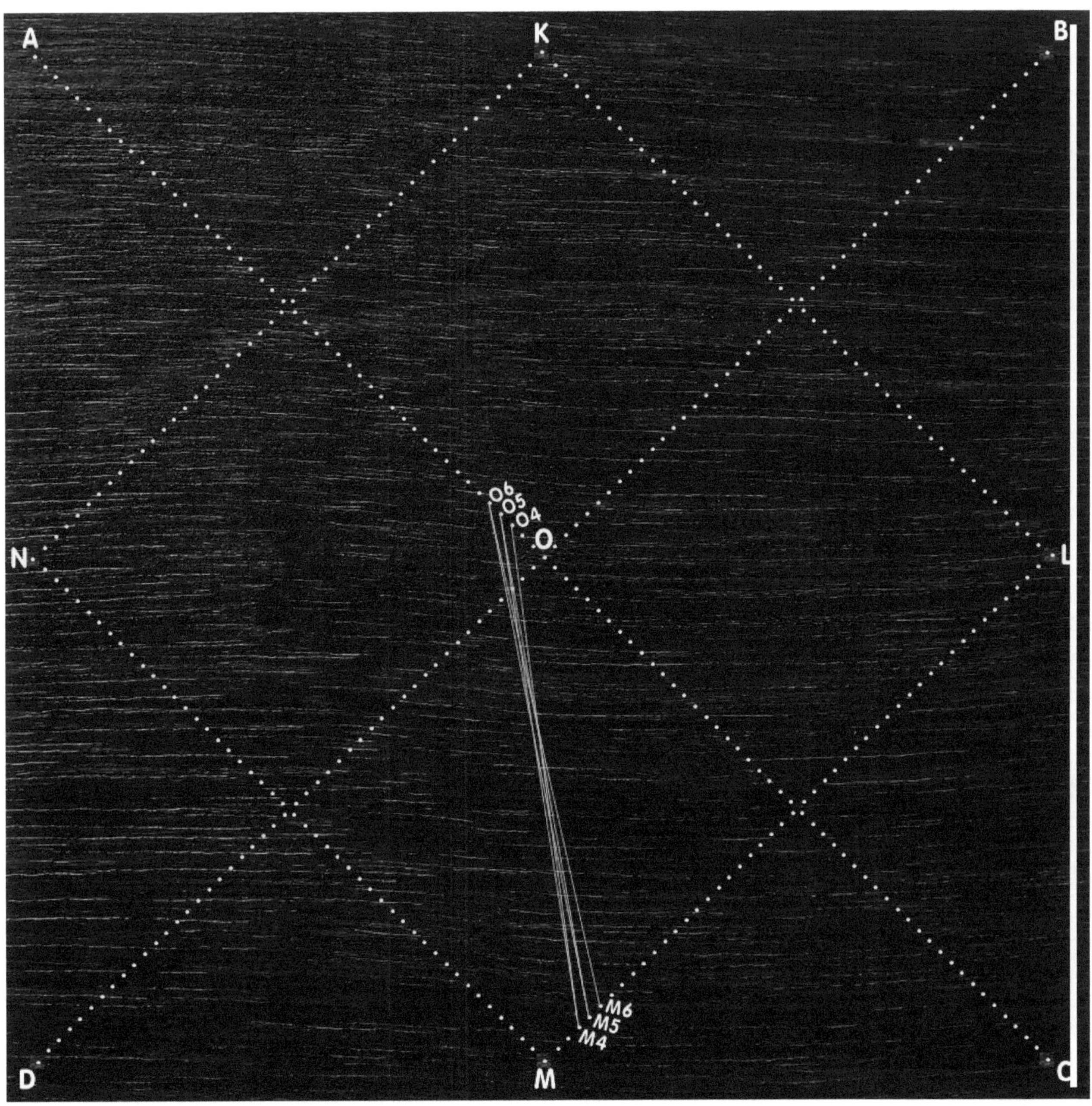

Continue this step until you reach the nail-point O19 from point-O and the nail-point M19 from Point-M. Tie the string onto that nail and you will get the result as shown below:

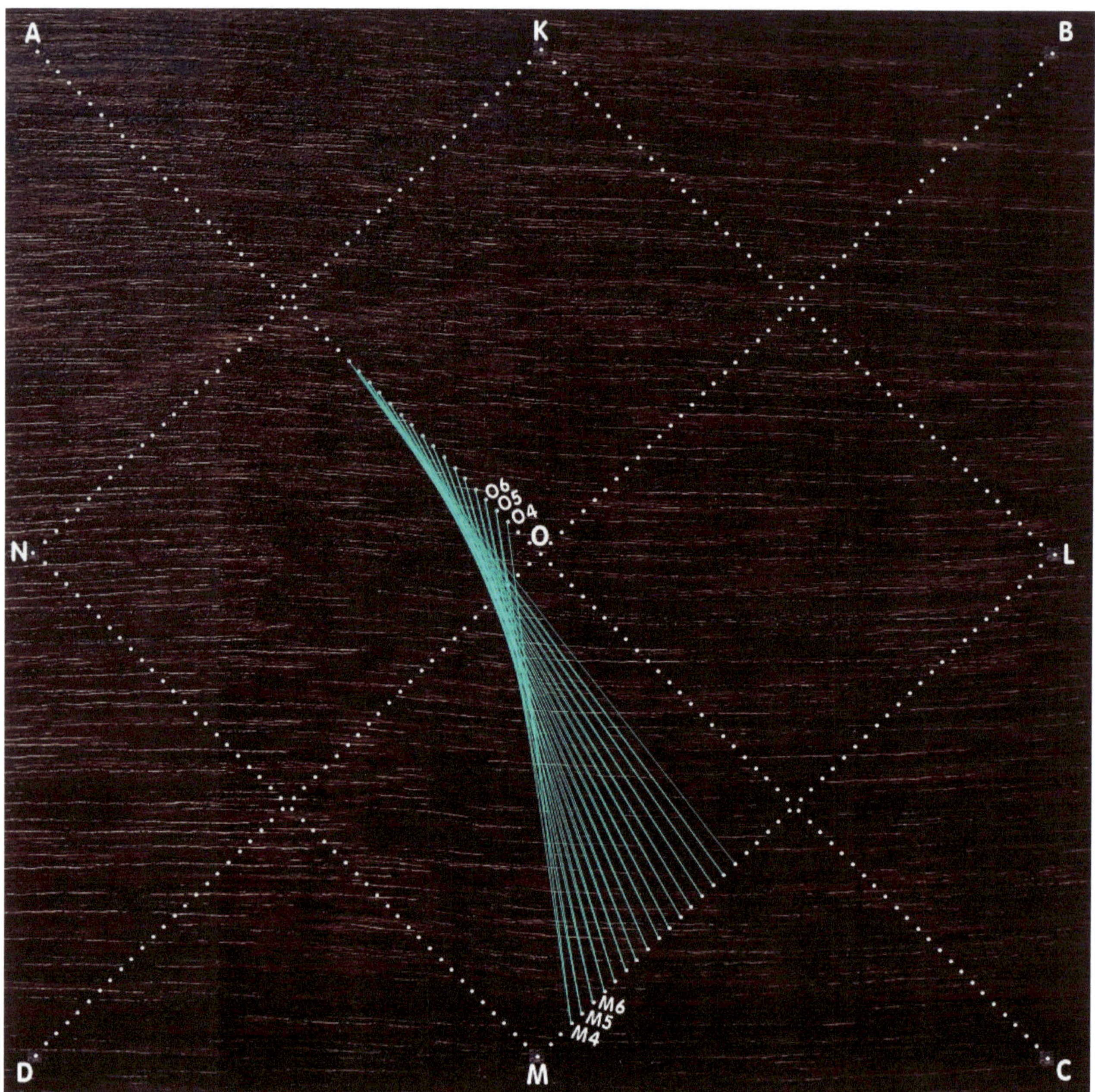

Repeat the same process in other side of the design and you will get the result as shown below:

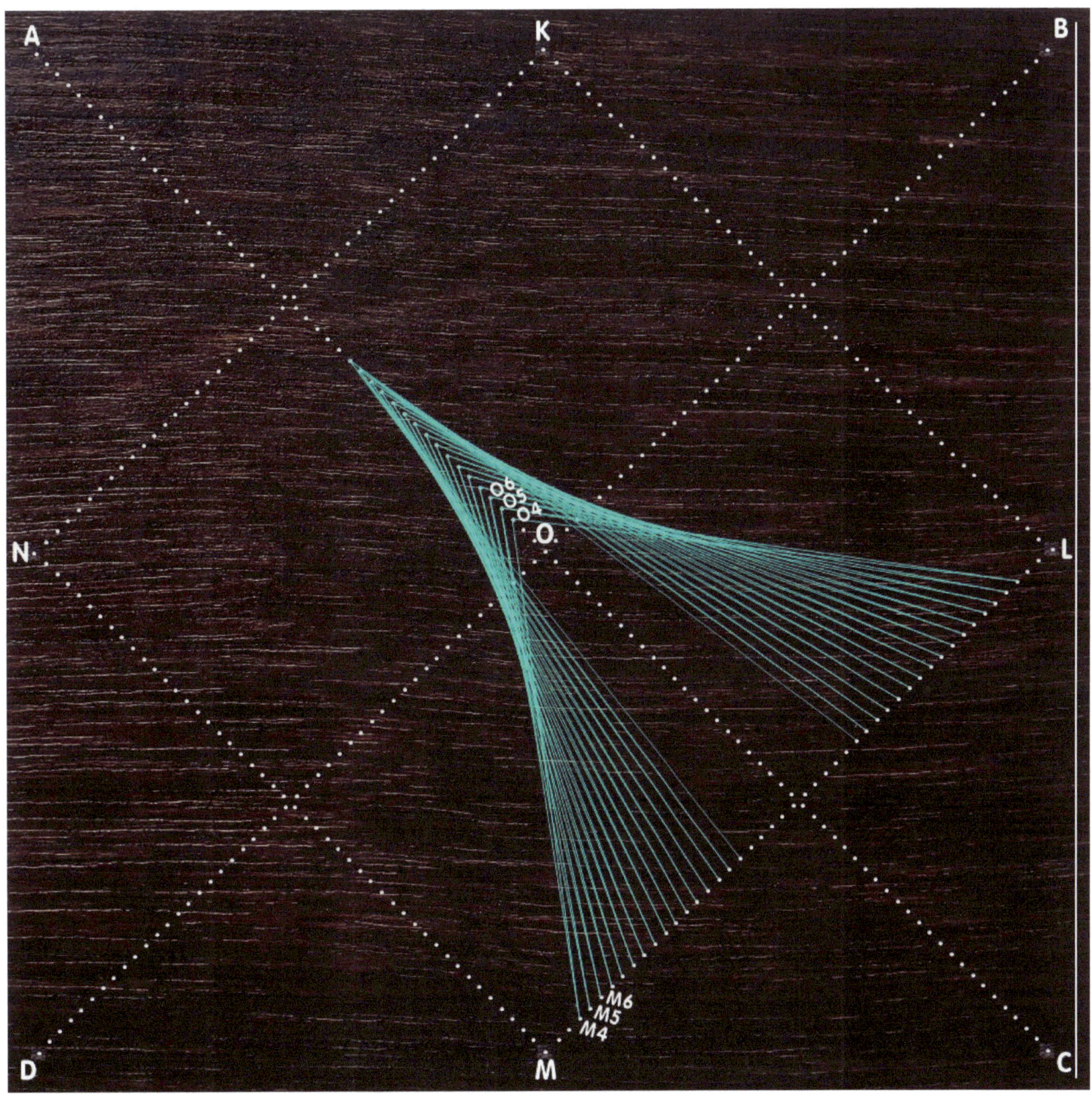

Repeat the same process in the left side (bottom) of the design and you will get the result as shown below:

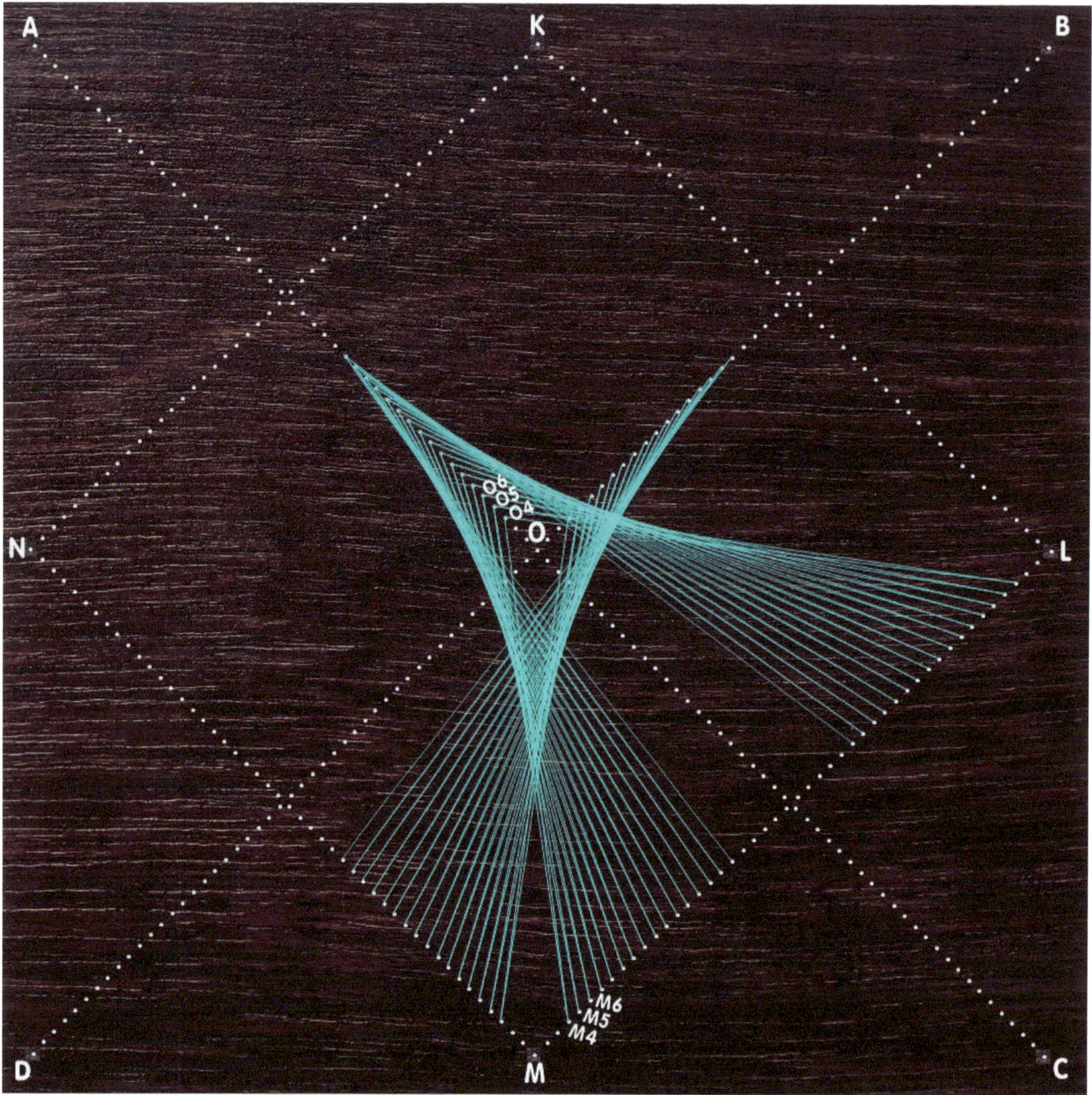

Also repeat the same process in the left side (top) of the design and you will get the result as shown below:

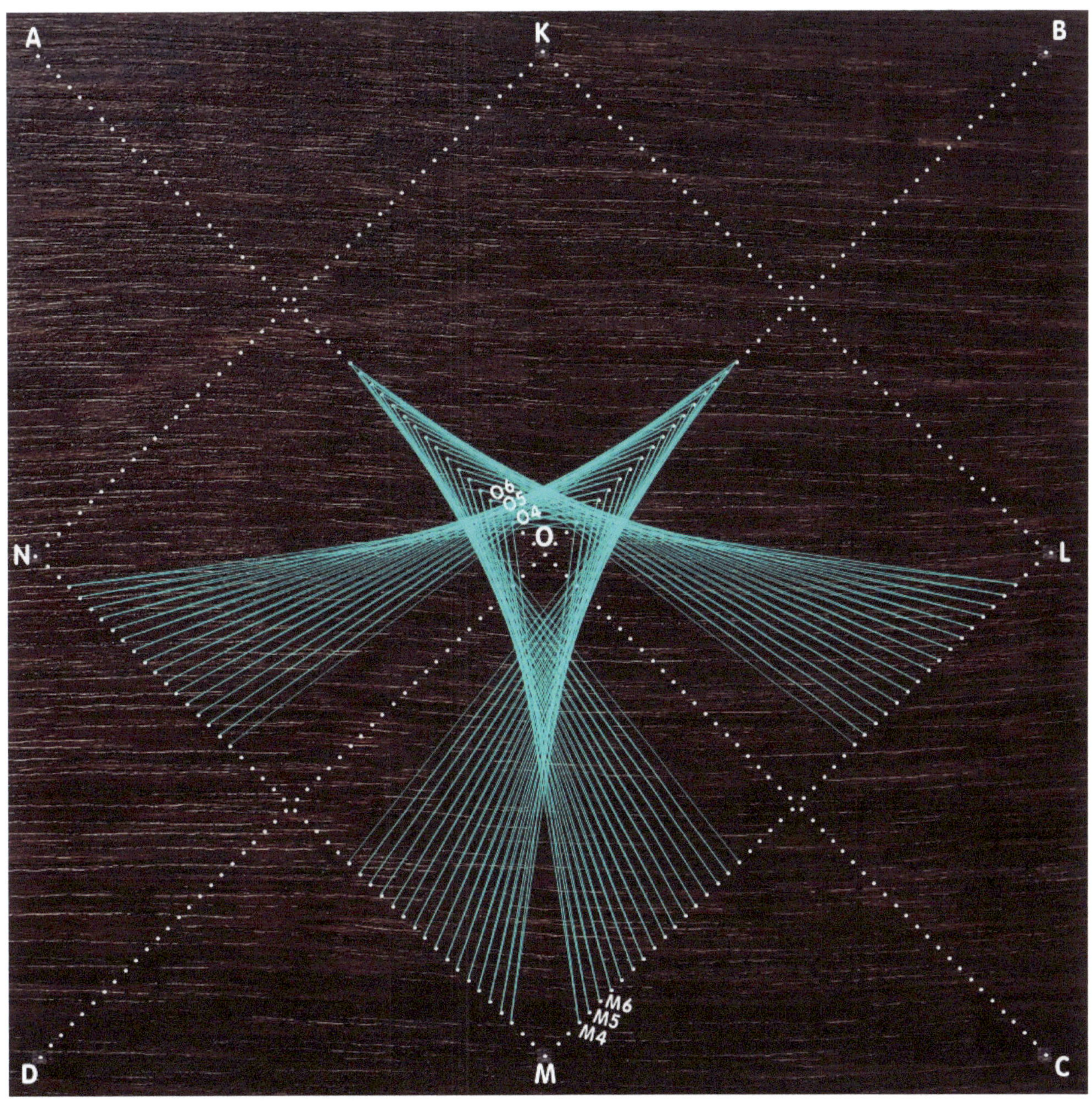

Also repeat the same process in all the sides and you will get the final result as shown below. This is the final result for Layer-3 in this design:

You will get the result as shown below once you have completed Layer-1, Layer-2 and Layer-3:

Final Result:

It may not look good in these diagrams but it is really beautiful when you make it real:

Different color:

You can also use different colors for making the same design:

OTHER STRING ART PROJECTS

Search the following code in Amazon to purchase the step by step instructions for the string art shown below:

For E-Book: B09CNS3RCH

For Premium quality color Paperback: B09CRSNMT8

Search the following code in Amazon to purchase the step by step instructions for the string art shown below:

For E-Book: B09CVSL8BT

For Premium quality color Paperback: B09CRY7N3K

Search the following code in Amazon to purchase the step by step instructions for the string art shown below:

For E-Book: B09D7JMN11

For Premium quality color Paperback: **B09CRTMFRT**

Search the following code in Amazon to purchase the step by step instructions for the string art shown below:

For E-Book: B09FYBDFZ4

For Premium quality color Paperback: B09FSCGXRL

COMING SOON